P · O · C · K · E · T · S

ESSENTIAL
FACTS

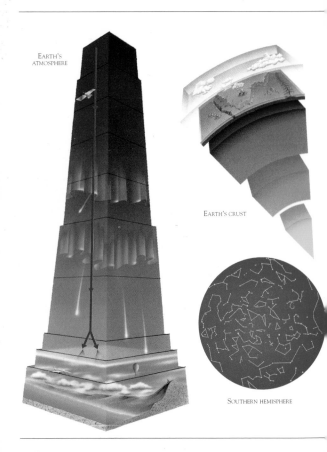

EARTH'S
ATMOSPHERE

EARTH'S CRUST

SOUTHERN HEMISPHERE

P · O · C · K · E · T · S

ESSENTIAL
FACTS

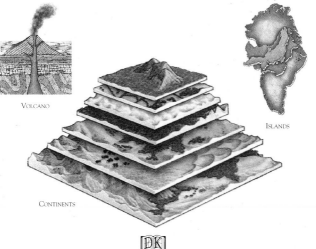

VOLCANO

ISLANDS

CONTINENTS

DK

A DK PUBLISHING BOOK

Project editors	Tim Hetherington
	Esther Labi
Designer	Janet Allis
Art editor	Clair Watson
Design assistant	Andrea Jeffrey-Hall
Senior editor	Alastair Dougall
Senior art editor	Sarah Crouch
Picture research	Sam Ruston
Production	Josie Alabaster
	Katie Holmes
US editor	Constance M. Robinson

First American Edition, 1996
2 4 6 8 10 9 7 5 3 1
Published in the United States by
DK Publishing, Inc., 95 Madison Avenue
New York, New York 10016

Published in Great Britain by Dorling Kindersley Ltd.
Distributed by Houghton Mifflin Company, Boston.

Library of Congress Cataloging-in-Publication Data

ISBN 0 7894 1020 6

Color reproduction by Colourscan, Singapore
Printed and bound in Italy by L.E.G.O.

CONTENTS

HOW TO USE THIS BOOK

These pages show you how to use *Pockets: Essential Facts*. The book is divided into six sections. These cover all the essential subjects, ranging from the solar system to world religion to mathematics. At the beginning of each section there is a picture page and a guide to the contents of that particular section.

HEADING
The heading describes the overall subject of the page. This page is about water.

INTRODUCTION
The introduction provides an overview of the subject. After reading this, you should have a clear idea of what the following page, or pages, are about.

CORNER CODING
The corners of the main section pages are color-coded to remind you which section you are in.

- ▪ THE WORLD AROUND US
- ▪ THE POLITICAL WORLD
- ▪ TECHNOLOGY
- ▪ SCIENCE
- ▪ MATHEMATICS
- ▪ PEOPLE

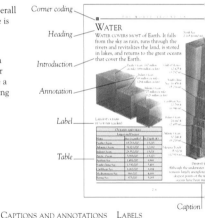

Corner coding

Heading

Introduction

Annotation

Label

Table

Caption

CAPTIONS AND ANNOTATIONS
Each illustration carries an explanatory caption. Some also have annotations, in *italics*. These point out the features of an illustration, and often use leader lines.

LABELS
For clarity, some pictures have labels. These give extra information about the picture, or may provide clearer identification.

RUNNING HEADS

These remind you which section you are in. The top of the left-hand page gives the section name, and the top of the right-hand page gives the subject heading.

FACT BOXES

Many pages have fact boxes. These provide at-a-glance information about the subject, such as how much water flows from the Amazon.

MAPS

Some pages in the book contain maps. These have annotations and labels to aid identification and give further information.

Running head

Fact box

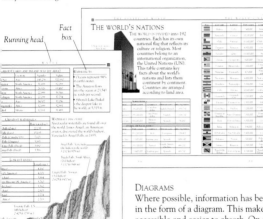

DIAGRAMS

Where possible, information has been presented in the form of a diagram. This makes data more accessible and easier to absorb. On these pages, for example, the volumes of the greatest oceans are shown as an illustration.

TABLES

Tables give comparative data listings for particular subject examples. On these pages, the relative sizes of aquatic features are listed in numerical order.

INDEX

At the back of the book, there is an index. It lists alphabetically every subject included in the book. By referring to the index, the reader can find information on particular topics.

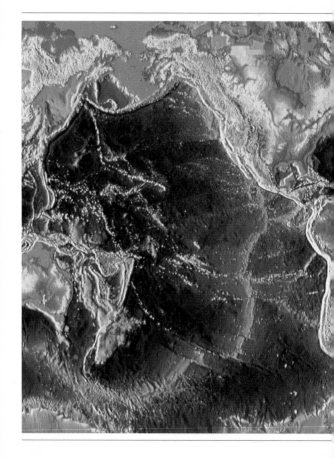

THE WORLD AROUND US

THE NIGHT SKY

STARS, OF WHICH OUR SUN is an example, are scattered throughout the universe. Ancient people observed their patterns in the night sky as different groups, or constellations. For thousands of years, navigators have used the stars as guides.

CONSTELLATIONS OF
THE NORTHERN
HEMISPHERE

Betelgeuse,
a huge star in the
known universe,
is 400 times
larger than
the Sun

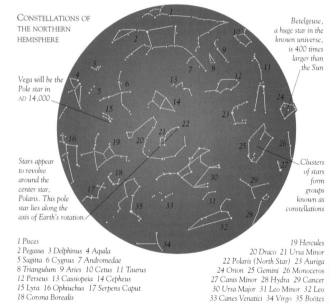

Vega will be the
Pole star in
AD 14,000

Stars appear
to revolve
around the
center star,
Polaris. This pole
star lies along the
axis of Earth's rotation

Clusters
of stars
form
groups
known as
constellations

1 Pisces
2 Pegasus 3 Delphinus 4 Aquila
5 Sagitta 6 Cygnus 7 Andromedae
8 Triangulum 9 Aries 10 Cetus 11 Taurus
12 Perseus 13 Cassiopeia 14 Cepheus
15 Lyra 16 Ophiuchus 17 Serpens Caput
18 Corona Borealis

19 Hercules
20 Draco 21 Ursa Minor
22 Polaris (North Star) 23 Auriga
24 Orion 25 Gemini 26 Monoceros
27 Canis Minor 28 Hydra 29 Cancer
30 Ursa Major 31 Leo Minor 32 Leo
33 Canes Venatici 34 Virgo 35 Boötes

THE MILKY WAY

The Sun is one of the 200 billion stars in our galaxy, the Milky Way. Scientists believe we belong to a spiral-style galaxy with a diameter of 100,000 light years. Because of the solar system's position in the Orion arm of the spiral, we view the Milky Way as a luminous band of bright stars without the spiral details.

MILKY WAY WITH METEOR STREAK   Milky Way

CONSTELLATIONS OF
THE SOUTHERN
HEMISPHERE

Stars near the edge
become visible
month by
month
through
the year

Sirius is the
brightest star in
the night sky

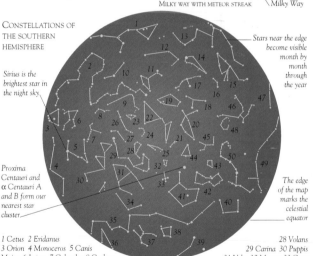

Proxima
Centauri and
α Centauri A
and B form our
nearest star
cluster

The edge
of the map
marks the
celestial
equator

1 Cetus 2 Eridanus
3 Orion 4 Monoceros 5 Canis
Major 6 Lepus 7 Columba 8 Caelum
9 Horologium 10 Fornax 11 Phoenix 12 Sculptor
13 Aquarius 14 Piscis Austrinus 15 Capricornus
16 Microscopium 17 Grus 18 Indus 19 Tucana
20 Pavo 21 Apus 22 Hydrus 23 Reticulum
24 Mensa 25 Chameleon 26 Dorado 27 Pictor

28 Volans
29 Carina 30 Puppis
31 Vela 32 Mucsa 33 Crux
34 Antila 35 Hydra 36 Sextans 37 Crater
38 Corvus 39 Virgo 40 Libra 41 Centaurus
42 Lupus 43 Norma 44 Triangulum Australe
45 Ara 46 Sagittarius 47 Aquila 48 Corona
Australis 49 Ophiuchus 50 Scorpius

THE SUN AND MOON

OUR CLOSEST STAR, the Sun, is a spinning ball of gas.
Nuclear reactions take place in its core, creating heat
and light. The Moon revolves around
Earth in its orbit of the Sun.

THE SUN

- Diameter: 865,000 miles (1,392,000 km)
- Time taken to orbit galaxy: 240 million years
- Distance from Earth: 92.9 million miles (149.6 million km)
- Surface temperature: 9,900°F (5,500°C)
- Life expectancy: 10 billion years
- Age: 5 million years
- Mass (Earth =1): 332,946

WHAT IS A SOLAR ECLIPSE?
Occasionally the Moon
becomes precisely aligned
between the Sun and
Earth. Viewed from parts
of Earth, the Moon covers
the disc of the Sun
perfectly. This blocks the
light and causes a brief
period of darkness known
as a solar eclipse.

TOTAL SOLAR ECLIPSES (1996–2006)	
DATE	WHERE VISIBLE
Mar. 9, 1997	Siberia, Arctic
Feb. 26, 1998	Mid-Pacific, C. America, N. Atlantic
Aug. 11, 1999	N. Atlantic, N. Europe, Middle East, N. India
June 21, 2001	S. America, S. Atlantic, S. Africa, Pacific
Dec. 4, 2002	Mid-Atlantic, S. Africa, S. Pacific, Australia
Nov. 23, 2003	S. Pacific, Antarctic
Apr. 8, 2005	Pacific, Panama, Venezuela
Mar. 29, 2006	Atlantic, Libya, Turkey, Russia

SOLAR ECLIPSE

Sun   Moon   Penumbra   Umbra   Earth

THE MOON, AS SEEN FROM SPACE

THE MOON

- Diameter: 2,160 miles (3,476 km)
- Age: 4.6 billion years
- Distance from Earth: 238,000 miles (384,000 km)
- Surface temperature: −247/ 221°F (−155°C/ 105°C)
- The Moon spins on its axis at the same rate that it orbits Earth, so the same side is always visible.
- The pull of the Moon's gravity is largely responsible for the rise and fall of tides on Earth.

THE PHASES OF THE MOON

| NEW MOON | CRESCENT | FIRST QUARTER | GIBBOUS | FULL MOON | GIBBOUS | LAST QUARTER | CRESCENT |

WHAT IS A LUNAR ECLIPSE?

Occasionally Earth becomes perfectly aligned between the Sun and the Moon. When this happens, Earth blocks light from the Sun and cast its shadow across the Moon. Viewed from Earth, this shadow crossing the Moon is known as a lunar eclipse.

TOTAL LUNAR ECLIPSES (1996–2006)	
DATE	WHERE VISIBLE
Apr. 4, 1996	Africa, Europe, S. America
Sept. 27, 1996	C. and S. America, parts of N. America, W. Africa
Sept. 16, 1997	S. Africa, E. Africa, Australia
Jan. 21, 2000	N. America, parts of S. America, S.W. Europe
July 16, 2000	Pacific, Australia, S.E. Asia
Jan. 9, 2001	Europe, Asia, Africa
May 16, 2003	N. America, C. and S. America, Europe, Africa
Nov. 9, 2003	N. America, C. and S. America, Africa, W. Asia
May. 4, 2004	Europe, Africa, Asia
Oct. 28, 2004	N. America, C. and S. America, Europe, Africa

LUNAR ECLIPSE

Earth   Umbra   Penumbra

Sun

Moon

THE PLANETS

Jupiter, the largest planet, could contain 1,300 Earths

A PLANET IS A BODY that orbits the Sun or any other star. The nine planets in our solar system divide into two groups. Mercury, Venus, Earth, and Mars form the dense and rocky inner planets. Jupiter, Saturn, Uranus, Neptune, and Pluto belong to the gaseous or icy outer ones.

MARS

JUPITER

Mercury has the fastest orbiting speed around the Sun

VENUS

EARTH

The planet's red color is caused by iron oxide

MERCURY

Venus has thick clouds of sulfuric acid

Inner and outer planets are separated by an asteroid belt

Sun   Earth

Mercury   Venus   Mars   Jupiter   Saturn

INNER PLANETS				
	MERCURY	VENUS	EARTH	MARS
DISTANCE FROM THE SUN IN MILLION MILES (MILLION KM)	36.0 (57.9)	67.2 (108.2)	93 (149.6)	141.6 (227.9)
DIAMETER IN MILES (KM)	3,031 (4,878)	7,520 (12,103)	7,926 (12,756)	4,217 (6,786)
TIME TAKEN TO ORBIT THE SUN	87.97 DAYS	224.70 DAYS	365.26 DAYS	686.98 DAYS
TIME TAKEN TO TURN ON AXIS	58 DAYS 16 HOURS	243 DAYS 14 HOURS	23 HOURS 56 MINS	24 HOURS 37 MINS
SURFACE TEMPERATURE	−292 TO 806°F (−180 TO 430°C)	869°F (465°C)	−94 TO 131°F (−70 TO 55°C)	−184 TO 77°F (−120 TO 25°C)
NUMBER OF MOONS	NONE	NONE	1	2
MASS (EARTH = 1)	0.055	0.81	1	0.11
DENSITY (WATER = 1)	5.43	5.25	5.52	3.95

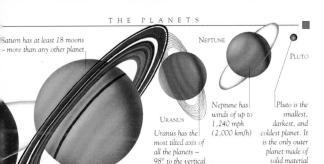

Saturn has at least 18 moons – more than any other planet

NEPTUNE

PLUTO

Pluto is the smallest, darkest, and coldest planet. It is the only outer planet made of solid material

Neptune has winds of up to 1,240 mph (2,000 km/h)

URANUS

Uranus has the most tilted axis of all the planets – 98° to the vertical

SATURN

Saturn's rings consist of ice-covered rock and dust particles. Saturn has the lowest density of all the planets: set on a huge lake, it would float

PLANETARY ORBITS
The Sun's huge gravitational pull holds the solar system together, forcing the planets to circle the Sun. The orbits of the four inner planets lie close to the Sun. Mercury, the nearest planet to the Sun, is 100 times closer than Pluto.

Uranus   Neptune   Pluto

OUTER PLANETS				
JUPITER	SATURN	URANUS	NEPTUNE	PLUTO
483.6 (778.3)	886 (1,427)	1,784 (2,871)	2,794 (4,497)	3,675 (5,914)
88,846 (142,984)	74,898 (120,536)	31,763 (51,118)	30,775 (49,528)	1,419 (2,284)
11.86 YEARS	29.46 YEARS	84.01 YEARS	164.79 YEARS	248.54
9 HOURS 55 MINS	10 HOURS 40 MINS	17 HOURS 14 MINS	16 HOURS 7 MINS	6 DAYS 9 HOURS
−238°F (−150°C) AT CLOUD TOPS	−292°F (−180°C) AT CLOUD TOPS	−346°F (−210°C) AT CLOUD TOPS	−346°F (−210°C) AT CLOUD TOPS	−364°F (−220°C)
16	18	15	8	1
318	95.18	14.5	17.14	0.0022
1.33	0.69	1.29	1.64	2.03

PLANET EARTH

OF ALL THE PLANETS, only Earth has the necessary ingredients for life. Because of its unique position in the solar system, all aspects of the environment are regulated, from the seasonal cycles to the oceans tides.

THE SEASONS
Earth orbits the Sun with a tilt of 23.5°. This mechanism causes a rotation of seasons. When the northern hemisphere tilts towards the Sun, it experiences summer, and the south, winter. As the orbit changes, so the seasons change.

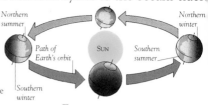

Northern summer

Northern winter

Path of Earth's orbit

SUN

Southern summer

Southern winter

EARTH

- Diameter: 7,926 miles (12,756 km) at equator, 7,899 miles (12,713 km) at poles
- Age: 4.6 billion years old
- Distance from the Sun: 93 million miles (150 milllion km)
- Mass: 59,760 trillion tons
- Area: 29.2% land, 70.8% water
- Orbiting time: 365.26 days
- Orbiting speed: 18.5 miles/sec (29.8 km /sec)

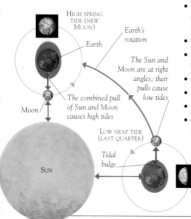

HIGH SPRING TIDE (NEW MOON)

Earth's rotation

Earth

The Sun and Moon are at right angles; their pulls cause low tides

Moon

The combined pull of Sun and Moon causes high tides

LOW NEAP TIDE (LAST QUARTER)

Tidal bulge

SUN

HOW TIDES ARE FORMED
Gravity from the Sun and Moon cause the cycle of ocean tides on Earth. High, low, and neap tides all result when configurations of the Sun and Moon pull on the rotating Earth.

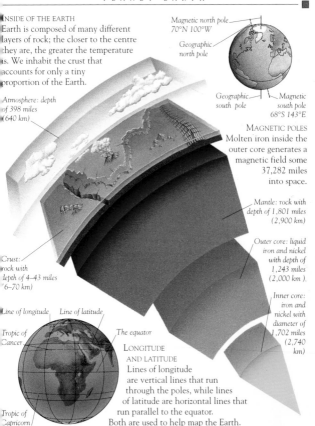

INSIDE OF THE EARTH
Earth is composed of many different layers of rock; the closer to the centre they are, the greater the temperature is. We inhabit the crust that accounts for only a tiny proportion of the Earth.

Atmosphere: depth of 398 miles (640 km)

Magnetic north pole
70°N 100°W

Geographic north pole

Geographic south pole

Magnetic south pole
68°S 143°E

MAGNETIC POLES
Molten iron inside the outer core generates a magnetic field some 37,282 miles into space.

Mantle: rock with depth of 1,801 miles (2,900 km)

Outer core: liquid iron and nickel with depth of 1,243 miles (2,000 km).

Crust: rock with depth of 4–43 miles (6–70 km)

Inner core: iron and nickel with diameter of 1,702 miles (2,740 km)

Line of longitude   *Line of latitude*

Tropic of Cancer

The equator

Tropic of Capricorn

LONGITUDE AND LATITUDE
Lines of longitude are vertical lines that run through the poles, while lines of latitude are horizontal lines that run parallel to the equator. Both are used to help map the Earth.

More about the Earth

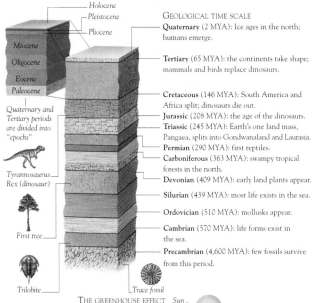

Holocene
Pleistocene
Pliocene
Miocene
Oligocene
Eocene
Paleocene

Quaternary and Tertiary periods are divided into "epochs"

Tyrannosaurus Rex (dinosaur)

First tree

Trilobite

Trace fossil

GEOLOGICAL TIME SCALE

Quaternary (2 MYA): Ice ages in the north; humans emerge.

Tertiary (65 MYA): the continents take shape; mammals and birds replace dinosaurs.

Cretaceous (146 MYA): South America and Africa split; dinosaurs die out.

Jurassic (208 MYA): the age of the dinosaurs.

Triassic (245 MYA): Earth's one land mass, Pangaea, splits into Gondwanaland and Laurasia.

Permian (290 MYA): first reptiles.

Carboniferous (363 MYA): swampy tropical forests in the north.

Devonian (409 MYA): early land plants appear.

Silurian (439 MYA): most life exists in the sea.

Ordovician (510 MYA): mollusks appear.

Cambrian (570 MYA): life forms exist in the sea.

Precambrian (4,600 MYA): few fossils survive from this period.

THE GREENHOUSE EFFECT

Pollutant gases, such as carbon dioxide, act like glass in a greenhouse. They let the Sun's rays in but prevent excess heat from escaping from Earth's surface. This process, known as global warming, can cause temperatures to rise. Scientists predict that the temperature on Earth could rise by as much as 7°F (4°C) by the year 2050.

Sun

Heat escapes into space

Reflected heat

Solar radiation

Gases trapped in atmosphere

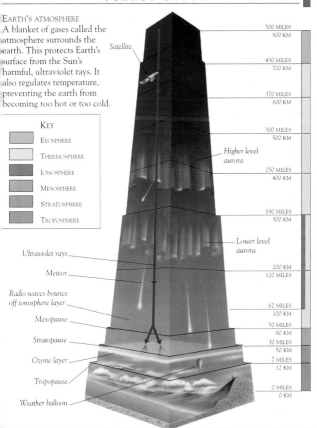

EARTH'S ATMOSPHERE
A blanket of gases called the atmosphere surrounds the earth. This protects Earth's surface from the Sun's harmful, ultraviolet rays. It also regulates temperature, preventing the earth from becoming too hot or too cold.

Satellite

KEY

- EXOSPHERE
- THERMOSPHERE
- IONOSPHERE
- MESOSPHERE
- STRATOSPHERE
- TROPOSPHERE

Higher level aurora

Lower level aurora

Ultraviolet rays

Meteor

Radio waves bounce off ionosphere layer

Mesopause

Stratopause

Ozone layer

Tropopause

Weather balloon

500 MILES / 800 KM
430 MILES / 700 KM
370 MILES / 600 KM
300 MILES / 500 KM
250 MILES / 400 KM
190 MILES / 300 KM
200 KM / 120 MILES
62 MILES / 100 KM
50 MILES / 80 KM
30 KM / 50 KM
7 MILES / 12 KM
0 MILES / 0 KM

WORLD TIME ZONES

THE EARTH IS divided into 24 time zones, one for each hour of the day. Greenwich, in southeast London, England, is on the 0° meridian. Time advances by one hour for every 15° of longitude east of Greenwich.

TIME ZONES
The numbers on the map indicate the number of hours that must be subtracted or added to reach GMT. When it is noon at Greenwich, for example, it is 10 p.m. in Sydney, Australia. Time zones are adjusted to regional administrative boundaries.

KEY TO MAP

⬤ MINUS HOURS

⬤ PLUS HOURS

◯ GREENWICH MEAN TIME

⬤ DATE LINE

▦ TIME ZONES

GMT
Greenwich Mean Time (GMT) is the exact time in Greenwich, London. Clocks are set depending on whether they are east or west of Greenwich.

INTERNATIONAL DATE LINE
The International Date Line is an imaginary line that runs along the 180° meridian but deviates around countries.

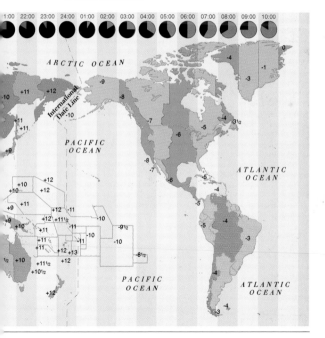

THE PHYSICAL WORLD

LAND ACCOUNTS FOR just over a quarter of the earth's total surface area. This comprises seven principal landmasses, known as the continents. Each continent features a variety of landscapes, such as mountains, deserts, forests, and pasturelands.

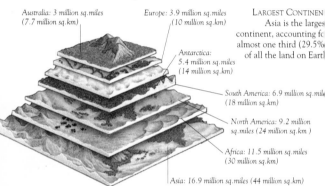

Australia: 3 million sq.miles (7.7 million sq.km)

Europe: 3.9 million sq.miles (10 million sq.km)

Antarctica: 5.4 million sq.miles (14 million sq.km)

South America: 6.9 million sq.miles (18 million sq.km)

North America: 9.2 million sq.miles (24 million sq.km)

Africa: 11.5 million sq.miles (30 million sq.km)

Asia: 16.9 million sq.miles (44 million sq.km)

LARGEST CONTINENT
Asia is the largest continent, accounting for almost one third (29.5%) of all the land on Earth.

HIGH AND LOW POINTS AROUND THE WORLD				
NAME OF CONTINENT	HIGHEST POINT ABOVE SEA LEVEL	HEIGHT IN FEET (METERS)	LOWEST POINT BELOW SEA LEVEL	DEPTH IN FEET (METERS)
Asia	Mt. Everest	29,030/8,848	Dead Sea	−1,312 (−400)
Africa	Kilimanjaro	19,341 (5,895)	Qattâra Depression	−436 (−133)
N. America	Denali (Mt. McKinley)	20,323 (6,194)	Death Valley	−282 (−86)
S. America	Aconcagua	22,836 (6,960)	Peninsular Valdez	−131 (−40)
Antarctica	Vinson Massif	16,864 (5,140)	Bentley Subglacial Trench	−8,327(−2,538)
Europe	Elbrus	18,511 (5,642)	Caspian Sea	−92 (−28)
Australia	Mt. Kosciusko	7,310 (2,228)	Lake Eyre	−52 (−16)

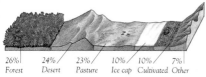

| 26% Forest | 24% Desert | 23% Pasture | 10% Ice cap | 10% Cultivated | 7% Other |

DIVISION OF THE EARTH'S LAND AREA

The total surface area of the earth is about 196 million square miles, of which only 57 million square miles is land. Of this, over half is either abundant forest or inhospitable desert.

LARGEST DESERTS	AREA: SQ.MILES (SQ.KM)
Sahara Desert (Africa)	3,500,000 (9,065,000)
Arabian Desert (Asia)	502,000 (1,300,000)
Gobi Desert (Asia)	402,000 (1,040,000)
Kalahari Desert (Africa)	224,000 (580,000)
Great Sandy Desert (Australia)	160,000 (414,000)
Chihuahuan Desert (N. America)	143,000 (370,000)
Takla Makan Desert (Asia)	198,848 (320,000)
Kara Kum Desert (Asia)	120,000 (310,000)
Namib Desert (Africa)	120,000 (310,000)
Thar Desert (Asia)	100,000 (260,000)

HIGHEST MOUNTAINS

The 10 highest peaks are all found in the Himalaya mountain range, which lies between Tibet/China and the Indian subcontinent.

Borneo: 287,422 sq.miles (744,366 sq.km)

Honshu, Japan: 88,983 sq.miles (230,448 sq.km)

Greenland: 840,065 sq.miles (2,175,600 sq.km)

LARGEST ISLANDS

Greenland is the world's largest island (Australia is considered a continent). It is three times as big as Borneo, the second largest island in the world, and nine times the size of Honshu, Japan's largest island.

Everest: 29,028 ft (8,848 m)

K2: 28,250 ft (8,611 m)

Kanchenjunga: 28,208 ft (8,597 m)

Lhotse I: 27,923 ft (8,511 m)

Makalu I: 27,824 ft (8,481 m)

WATER

WATER COVERS MOST of Earth. It falls from the sky as rain, runs through the rivers and revitalizes the land, is stored in lakes, and returns to the great oceans that cover Earth.

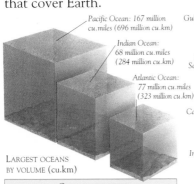

North Sea: 2,165 ft (660 m)

Pacific Ocean: 167 million cu.miles (696 million cu.km)

Indian Ocean: 68 million cu.miles (284 million cu.km)

Atlantic Ocean: 77 million cu.miles (323 million cu.km)

Gulf of Mexico: 12,425 ft (3,787 m)

South China Sea: 16,456 ft (5,016 m)

Caribbean Sea: 22,788 ft (6,946 m)

Indian Ocean: 24,660 ft (7,455 m)

Atlantic Ocean: 30,246 ft (9,219 m)

Mariana Trench: 35,820 ft (10,918 m)

LARGEST OCEANS BY VOLUME (cu.km)

OCEANS AND SEAS		
Largest and Deepest		
Name	Area (sq.miles)	Av. Depth (ft)
Pacific Ocean	63,783,000	13,215
Atlantic Ocean	31,821,000	12,880
Indian Ocean	28,352,000	13,001
Arctic Ocean	5,398,000	13,123
Arabian Sea	1,491,000	8,969
South China Sea	1,330,000	5,419
Caribbean Sea	1,062,000	8,684
Mediterranean Sea	966,000	4,688
Bering Sea	875,000	5,095

DEEPEST WATER
Although the underwater world remains largely unexplored, the deepest points of the world's oceans have been mapped.

LARGEST LAKES AND INLAND SEAS (BY AREA)

Lake	Location	Sq.miles	Sq.km
Caspian Sea	Asia	143,236	370,980
Lake Superior	North America	31,698	82,098
Lake Victoria	Africa	26,826	69,480
Lake Huron	North America	22,999	59,566
Lake Michigan	North America	22,299	57,754
Aral Sea	Asia	14,307	37,056
Lake Tanganyika	Africa	12,699	32,891
Lake Baikal	Siberia	12,161	31,498

WATER FACTS

• Oceans represent 94% of earth's water.

• The Amazon flows into the ocean at 23,543 cu. yards per second.

• Siberia's Lake Baikal is the deepest lake in the world, at 5,315 ft.

GREATEST WATERFALLS

Name	Flow (cu.yd/sec)
Boyoma Falls (Zaire)	22,235
Khône Falls (Laos)	15,185
Niagara Falls (Canada/ US)	7,625
Grande Falls (Uruguay)	5,885
Paulo Afonso Falls (Brazil)	3,780
Urubupungá Falls (Brazil)	3,596

LONGEST RIVERS

Name	Length (mi.)
Nile (Africa)	4,160
Amazon (S. America)	4,001
Yangtze (Asia)	3,964
Mississippi-Missouri (N. America)	3,710
Ob-Irtysh (Asia)	3,362
Yellow (Asia)	2,903
Amur (Asia)	2,774
Congo (Africa)	2,718

WATERFALL DISCOVERY

Spectacular waterfalls are found all over the world. James Angel, an American aviator, discovered the world's highest, Venezuela's Angel Falls, in 1935.

Angel Falls, Venezuela (the highest in the world) : 3,212 ft (979 m)

Tugela Falls, South Africa (2nd highest) : 3,110 ft (948 m)

Utigård Falls, Norway (3rd highest): 2,625 ft (800 m)

Yosemite Falls, US (4th highest): 2,425 ft (739 m)

Khône Falls, Laos (the world's widest waterfall): 6.7 miles (10.8 km)

THE EARTH'S CRUST

A LAYER OF ROCK known as the crust covers the earth.
Huge slabs called tectonic plates join to form this
protective layer. Movement occurs where these plates
meet, and this may cause volcanoes, mountains, deep-
sea trenches, fault lines, and earthquakes to develop.

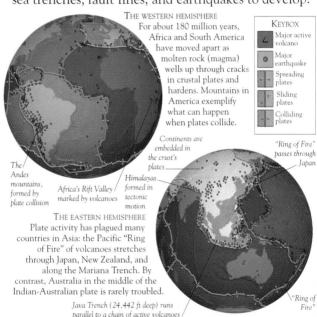

THE WESTERN HEMISPHERE
For about 180 million years,
Africa and South America
have moved apart as
molten rock (magma)
wells up through cracks
in crustal plates and
hardens. Mountains in
America exemplify
what can happen
when plates collide.

KEYBOX

△	Major active volcano
●	Major earthquake
	Spreading plates
	Sliding plates
	Colliding plates

*Continents are
embedded in
the crust's
plates*

*"Ring of Fire"
passes through
Japan*

*The
Andes
mountains,
formed by
plate collision*

*Africa's Rift Valley
marked by volcanoes*

*Himalayas
formed in
tectonic
motion*

THE EASTERN HEMISPHERE
Plate activity has plagued many
countries in Asia: the Pacific "Ring
of Fire" of volcanoes stretches
through Japan, New Zealand, and
along the Mariana Trench. By
contrast, Australia in the middle of the
Indian-Australian plate is rarely troubled.

*Java Trench (24,442 ft deep) runs
parallel to a chain of active volcanoes*

*"Ring of
Fire"*

MAJOR ACTIVE VOLCANOES		
NAME	HEIGHT(FT)	LAST ERUPTION
Nyamuragira, Zaire	10,016	1989
Mt. Cameroon, Cameroon	13,353	1982
Erebus, Antarctica	12,448	1989
Kliuchevskoi, Siberia	15,912	1990
Ruapehu, New Zealand	9,173	1989
Etna, Sicily, Italy	10,991	1992
Stromboli, Italy	3,038	1990
Mount St. Helens, US	8,363	1988
Mauna Loa, Hawaii	13,681	1984
Sangay, Ecuador	12,182	1989
Popocatepetl, Mexico	17,930	1943
Llullaillaco, Chile	22,057	1877

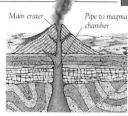

Main crater   Pipe to magma chamber

VOLCANO
Disturbances in the Earth's crust
can provoke volcanic activity.
This can force eruptions to
release molten rock from deep
inside the earth to the surface.

SEISMOMETERS
The Chinese first
devised an instrument
to detect earthquakes
in AD 132. Today,
ultrasensitive
machines
monitor
movements.

*Movement of
the earth is
measured vertically*

*Rotating graph
records activity*

MERCALLI AND RICHTER SCALES
Scientists measure the size of an
earthquake using two different scales.
The Richter scale is logarithmic and
measures magnitude; and the Modified
Mercalli Intensity scale measures the
actual effect on a descriptive
scale of I–XII.

MERCALLI SCALE	
XII	Total destruction; waves seen on ground surface; river courses altered.
XI	Railway tracks bend; roads break up; large cracks appear in ground; rock falls.
X	Most buildings destroyed; water thrown from rivers; large landslides.
IX	General panic; damage to foundations; large buildings collapse.
VIII	Car steering affected; chimneys fall; tree branches break.
VII	Difficult for people to stand; plaster, bricks, and tiles fall.
VI	People walk unsteadily; windows break; pictures fall.
V	Doors swing open; buildings tremble; small objects fall.
IV	Dishes rattle; standing cars rock; trees shake.
III	Vibrations felt indoors; hanging objects swing.
II	People may notice slight vibrations.
I	Vibrations recorded by instruments.

1   2   3   4   5   6   7   8 8.9

RICHTER SCALE

WORLD CLIMATE ZONES

THE MAIN INFLUENCES on an area's climate are its distance from a large body of water, its height above sea level, and its distance from the equator. Climate is usually classified according to rainfall and temperature. Both sunlight levels and rainfall are highest, and show least variation, at the equator.

POLAR
In polar regions, all water is frozen solid. Antarctica contains more than 80 percent of the world's fresh water as ice. The coldest temperature ever recorded here is −72°F (−57.8°C).

COOL
Polar air fronts bring cold temperatures over the mainland. Large areas of North America, northern Europe, and Russia/Siberia produce coniferous forests (taiga) that reflect this cool climate.

TEMPERATE
Hot, dry summers and damp winters characterize the temperate climates of midlatitude areas. Warm and moist westerly winds affect these areas most of the year.

Equatorial forests contain 50% of all plant and animal species

The Atacama Desert, Chile, has an average of only 0.02 in (0.51 mm) of rain a year

The average temperature of Manaus, Brazil, is 68°F (27°C)

DESERT AND DRY LANDS
Deserts have the driest and most extreme climate in the world. Cold ocean currents or warm and dry subsiding air both reduce rainfall. Areas in a rainshadow or far from the sea are also prone to desertification.

TROPICAL
Tropical climates are hot: average noonday temperatures vary by only 3.7°F (2°C). Large rain forests depend on rainfall all year round, while tropical grasslands like the African Savannah survive through dry and wet seasons.

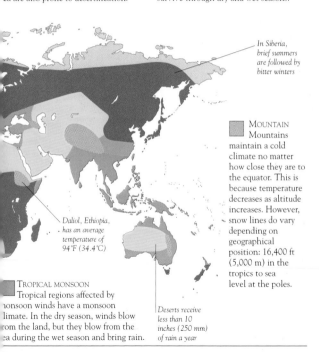

In Siberia, brief summers are followed by bitter winters

MOUNTAIN
Mountains maintain a cold climate no matter how close they are to the equator. This is because temperature decreases as altitude increases. However, snow lines do vary depending on geographical position: 16,400 ft (5,000 m) in the tropics to sea level at the poles.

Daliol, Ethiopia, has an average temperature of 94°F (34.4°C)

TROPICAL MONSOON
Tropical regions affected by monsoon winds have a monsoon climate. In the dry season, winds blow from the land, but they blow from the sea during the wet season and bring rain.

Deserts receive less than 10 inches (250 mm) of rain a year

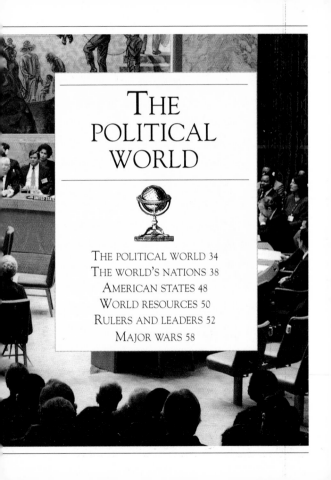

THE POLITICAL WORLD

THE POLITICAL WORLD

POLITICS IS THE SCIENCE of social organization. Every country in the world has a system of government that controls society and makes representative decisions. However, countries may have different political systems that reflect various methods of government, such as democracies, communist states, or military dictatorships.

MOST POPULATED COUNTRIES	
COUNTRY	TOTAL (MILLIONS)
China	1,192.0
India	934.2
US	263.1
Indonesia	192.5
Brazil	161.4
Russia	148.9
Pakistan	129.7

LEAST POPULATED COUNTRIES	
COUNTRY	TOTAL (MILLIONS)
Vatican City	750
Tuvalu	9,000
Nauru	9,500
San Marino	23,900
Liechtenstein	29,000
Monaco	30,000
St Kitts/ Nevis	44,000

This map shows population figures (in millions) for the world's main land areas and eight most populous cities.

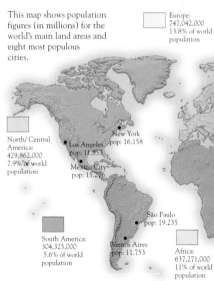

Europe:
747,042,000
13.8% of world
population

North/ Central America:
429,862,000
7.9% of world population

New York
pop: 16.158

Los Angeles
pop: 11.853

Mexico City
pop: 15.276

South America:
304,325,000
5.6% of world population

São Paulo
pop: 19.235

Buenos Aires
pop: 11.753

Africa:
637,271,000
11% of world population

LARGEST COUNTRIES

COUNTRY	AREA/MIL. SQ.MILES	MIL. SQ.KM
Russian Fed.	6.59	17.40
Canada	3.85	9.97
China	3.64	9.40
US	3.62	9.37
Brazil	3.29	8.51

SMALLEST COUNTRIES

COUNTRY	AREA/ SQ.MILES	SQ.KM
Vatican City	0.17	0.44
Monaco	0.75	1.95
Nauru	8.2	21.2
Tuvalu	10.0	26.0
San Marino	23.0	59.6

Tokyo
pop: 25.772

Shanghai
pop: 14.053

Bombay
pop: 13.322

Oceania:
27,229,000
0.5% of
world
population

Asia:
3,280,232,000
60.5% of world
population

WORLD ORGANIZATIONS

UNITED NATIONS
The United Nations
(UN) was set up in
1945 to address and
resolve global issues.

COMMONWEALTH
An association of
ex-British sovereign
states, its aims are
mutually beneficial.

EUROPEAN UNION
This council of
12 principal states
seeks economic
union in Europe.

NATO
After World War II,
the Allies created a
joint military force
for mutual purposes.

WHO
The World Health
Organization
monitors the well-
being of all people.

UNESCO
This is the UN's
educational,
scientific, and
cultural foundation.

RED CROSS
Founded in 1864,
the society offers
humanitarian aid
to all those in need.

RED CRESCENT
The Islamic
branch of the Red
Cross works in
Islamic countries.

Map of the world

THE WORLD'S NATIONS

UN HEADQUARTERS, NEW YORK

THE WORLD IS DIVIDED into 192 countries. Each has its own national flag that reflects its culture or religion. Most countries belong to an international organization, the United Nations (UN). This table contains key facts about the world's nations and lists them continent by continent. Countries are arranged according to land area.

NORTH AMERICA						
FLAG	COUNTRY	CAPITAL	POPULATION	CURRENCY	OFFICIAL LANG.	AREA (SQ MILES)
	Canada	Ottawa	28,200,000	Canadian dollar	English, French	3,851,790
	US	Washington, DC	255,200,000	United States dollar	English	3,618,760
	Mexico	Mexico City	88,200,000	Mexican new peso	Spanish	756,060
CENTRAL AND SOUTH AMERICA						
FLAG	COUNTRY	CAPITAL	POPULATION	CURRENCY	OFFICIAL LANG.	AREA (SQ MILES)
	Brazil	Brasilia	153,200,000	Real	Portuguese	3,286,470
	Argentina	Buenos Aires	33,100,000	Argentine peso	Spanish	1,068,300
	Peru	Lima	255,200,000	New sol	Spanish, Aymara, Quechua	496,220
	Colombia	Bogotá	33,400,000	Colombian peso	Spanish	439,730

Flag	Country	Capital	Population	Currency	Official lang.	Area (sq miles)
	Bolivia	La Paz	7,400,000	Boliviano	Spanish, Aymara, Quechua	424,160
	Venezuela	Caracas	20,200,000	Bolívar	Spanish	352,140
	Chile	Santiago	13,600,000	Chilean peso	Spanish	292,260
	Paraguay	Asunción	4,500,000	Guaraní	Spanish, Guaraní	157,050
	Ecuador	Quito	11,100,000	Sucre	Spanish	109,480
	Guyana	Georgetown	8,00,000	Guyana dollar	English	83,000
	Uruguay	Montevideo	3,100,000	Uruguayan peso	Spanish	68,500
	Suriname	Paramaribo	425,000	Suriname guilder	Dutch	63,040
	Nicaragua	Managua	4,000,000	New córdoba	Spanish	50,190
	Honduras	Tegucigalpa	5,500,000	Lempira	Spanish	43,280
	Cuba	Havana	10,800,000	Cuban peso	Spanish	42,800
	Guatemala	Guatemala City	9,200,000	Quetzal	Spanish	42,040
	Panama	Panama City	2,500,000	Balboa	Spanish	29,760
	Costa Rica	San José	3,200,000	Costa Rican dollar	Spanish	19,730
	Dominican Republic	Santo Domingo	7,500,000	Dominican Republic peso	Spanish	18,820
	Haiti	Port-au-Prince	6,500,000	Gourde	French, French Creole	10,710
	Belize	Belmopan	194,000	Belizean dollar	English	8,870
	El Salvador	San Salvador	5,400,000	Colón	Spanish	8,120
	Bahamas	Nassau	300,000	Bahamian dollar	English	5,360
	Jamaica	Kingston	2,500,000	Jamaican dollar	English	4,240
	Trinidad & Tobago	Port-of-Spain	1,300,000	Trinidad and Tobago dollar	English	1,980

Flag	Country	Capital	Population	Currency	Official lang.	Area (sq miles)
	Dominica	Roseau	83,000	East Caribbean dollar	English	290
	St. Lucia	Castries	153,000	East Caribbean dollar	English	239
	Antigua & Barbuda	St. John's	64,000	East Caribbean dollar	English	170
	Barbados	Bridgetown	300,000	Barbados dollar	English	166
	St Kitts & Nevis	Basseterre	44,000	East Caribbean dollar	English	139
	St. Vincent & the Grenadines	Kingstown	117,000	East Caribbean dollar	English	131
	Grenada	St George's	84,000	East Caribbean dollar	English	131

EUROPE						
Flag	Country	Capital	Population	Currency	Official lang.	Area (sq miles)
	Russian Federation	Moscow	148,700,000	Rouble	Russian	6,592,800
	Ukraine	Kiev	51,900,000	Karbovanets	Ukrainian	223,090
	France	Paris	57,200,000	Franc	French	212,930
	Spain	Madrid	39,100,000	Peseta	Spanish, Galician, Basque, Catalan	194,900
	Sweden	Stockholm	8,600,000	Swedish krona	Swedish	173,730
	Germany	Berlin	80,300,000	Deutsche Mark	German	137,800
	Finland	Helsinki	5,000,000	Markka	Finnish, Swedish	130,550
	Norway	Oslo	4,300,000	Norwegian krone	Norwegian	125,060
	Poland	Warsaw	38,400,000	Zloty	Polish	120,730
	Italy	Rome	57,800,000	Italian lira	Italian	116,320
	United Kingdom	London	57,700,000	Pound sterling	English	94,550
	Romania	Bucharest	23,300,000	Leu	Romanian	91,700
	Belorussia	Minsk	10,300,000	Belorussian rouble	Belorussian	80,150

Flag	Country	Capital	Population	Currency	Official lang.	Area (sq miles)
	Greece	Athens	10,200,000	Drachma	Greek	50,960
	Bulgaria	Sofia	9,000,000	Lev	Bulgarian	42,820
	Iceland	Reykjavík	300,000	New Icelandic króna	Icelandic	39,770
	Serbia	Belgrade	10,400,000	Dinar	Serbo-Croatian	9,930
	Hungary	Budapest	10,500,000	Forint	Hungarian (Magyar)	35,920
	Portugal	Lisbon	9,900,000	Escudo	Portuguese	35,670
	Austria	Vienna	7,800,000	Austrian schilling	German	32,380
	Czech Republic	Prague	10,300,000	Czech koruna	Czech	30,260
	Ireland	Dublin	3,500,000	Irish pound	Irish, English	27,140
	Latvia	Riga	2,700,000	Lats	Latvian	24,940
	Lithuania	Vilnius	3,800,000	Litas	Lithuanian	25,170
	Croatia	Zagreb	4,800,000	Kuna	Croatian	21,830
	Bosnia & Herzegovina	Sarajevo	4,200,000	Bosnian dinar	Serbo-Croatian	19,740
	Slovakia	Bratislava	5,300,000	Slovak koruna	Slovak	19,110
	Estonia	Tallinn	1,600,000	Kroon	Estonian	17,420
	Denmark	Copenhagen	5,200,000	Danish kroner	Danish	16,630
	Switzerland	Bern	6,800,000	Swiss franc	German, French, Italian	15,940
	Netherlands	Amsterdam, The Hague	15,200,000	Netherlands guilder	Dutch	14,410
	Moldova	Chisnau	4,400,000	Moldovan leu	Romanian	13,010
	Belgium	Brussels	10,000,000	Belgian franc	Dutch, French, German	12,780
	Albania	Tirana	3,300,000	New lek	Albanian	11,100

FLAG	COUNTRY	CAPITAL	POPULATION	CURRENCY	OFFICIAL LANG.	AREA (SQ MILES)
	Macedonia	Skopje	1,900,000	Macedonian denar	None	9,930
	Slovenia	Ljubljana	1,900,000	Tolar	Slovene	7,820
	Luxembourg	Luxembourg	400,000	Luxembourg franc	Letzeburgish	998
	Andorra	Andorra la Vella	58,000	French franc, Spanish peseta	Catalan	181
	Malta	Valletta	356,000	Maltese lira	Maltese, English	124
	Liechtenstein	Vaduz	29,000	Swiss franc	German	62
	San Marino	San Marino	22,000	Italian lira	Italian	24
	Monaco	Monaco	30,000	French franc	French	0.75
	Vatican City	Not applicable	1,000	Lira	Italian, Latin	0.17

			ASIA			
FLAG	COUNTRY	CAPITAL	POPULATION	CURRENCY	OFFICIAL LANG.	AREA (SQ MILES)
	China	Beijing	1,200,000,000	Yuan	Mandarin	3,628,170
	India	New Delhi	879,500,000	Rupee	Hindi, English	1,269,340
	Kazakhstan	Alma-Ata	17,000,000	Tenge	Kazakh	1,049,150
	Saudi Arabia	Riyadh	15,900,000	Saudi riyal	Arabic	830,000
	Indonesia	Jakarta	191,200,000	Rupiah	Bahasa Indonesia	735,360
	Iran	Tehran	61,600,000	Iranian rial	Farsi	636,290
	Mongolia	Ulan Bator	2,300,000	Tughrik	Khalkhar Mongolian	604,250
	Pakistan	Islamabad	124,800,000	Pakistani rupee	Urdu	309,370
	Turkey	Ankara	58,400,000	Turkish lira	Turkish	300,950
	Burma (Myanmar)	Rangoon (Yangon)	42,500,000	Kyat	Burmese (Myanmar)	261,200
	Afghanistan	Kabul	16,500,000	Afghani	Persian, Pashtu	251,770

FLAG	COUNTRY	CAPITAL	POPULATION	CURRENCY	OFFICIAL LANG.	AREA (SQ MILES)
	Yemen	Sana	12,500,000	Yemen rial, Yemen dinar	Arabic	203,850
	Thailand	Bangkok	56,100,000	Baht	Thai	198,120
	Turkmenistan	Ashgabad	3,900,000	Manat	Turkmen	188,460
	Uzbekistan	Tashkent	21,000,000	Som	Uzbek	439,730
	Iraq	Baghdad	19,300,000	Iraqi dinar	Arabic	169,240
	Japan	Tokyo	124,000,000	Yen	Japanese	145,870
	Malaysia	Kuala Lumpur	18,800,000	Ringgit	Malay	127,320
	Vietnam	Hanoi	67,800,000	New dông	Vietnamese	127,240
	Philippines	Manila	65,200,000	Philippine peso	Filipino, English	114,830
	Laos	Vientiane	4,300,000	Kip	Lao	91,430
	Oman	Muscat	1,600,000	Omani rial	Arabic	82,030
	Kyrgyzstan	Bishkek	4,500,000	Som	Kyrgyz	76,640
	Syria	Damascus	13,300,000	Syrian pound	Arabic	71,500
	Cambodia	Phnom Penh	8,800,000	Riel	Khmer	69,000
	Bangladesh	Dhaka	119,300,000	Taka	Bengali	55,600
	Tajikistan	Dushanbe	5,600,000	Rouble	Tajik	55,250
	Nepal	Kathmandu	20,600,000	Nepalese rupee	Nepali	54,360
	North Korea	Pyongyang	22,600,000	Won	Korean	46,540
	South Korea	Seoul	44,200,000	Won	Korean	38,230
	Jordan	Amman	4,300,000	Jordanian dinar	Arabic	34,440
	Azerbaijan	Baku	7,300,000	Manat	Azerbaijani	33,440

FLAG	COUNTRY	CAPITAL	POPULATION	CURRENCY	OFFICIAL LANG.	AREA (SQ MILES)
	United Arab Emirates	Abu Dhabi	1,900,000	UAE dirham	Arabic	32,300
	Georgia	Tbilisi	5,500,000	Coupon	Georgian	26,910
	Sri Lanka	Colombo	17,700,000	Sri Lanka rupee	Sinhalese	25,330
	Bhutan	Thimpu	1,600,000	Ngultrum	Dzongkha	18,150
	Taiwan	Taipei	20,800,000	New Taiwan dollar	Mandarin	13,970
	Armenia	Yerevan	3,500,000	Dram	Armenian	11,500
	Israel	Jerusalem	5,300,000	New shekel	Hebrew	7,990
	Kuwait	Kuwait City	2,100,000	Kuwaiti dinar	Arabic	6,880
	Qatar	Doha	500,000	Qatar riyal	Arabic	4,250
	Lebanon	Beirut	2,800,000	Lebanese pound	Arabic	4,020
	Cyprus	Nicosia	708,000	Cyprus pound (Turkish lira)	Greek (Turkish)	3,570
	Brunei	Bandar Seri Begawan	300,000	Brunei dollar	Malay	2,230
	Bahrain	Manama	500,000	Bahrain dinar	Arabic	263
	Singapore	Singapore City	2,900,000	Singapore dollar	Malay, Chinese, Tamil, English	239
	Maldives	Male'	223,000	Rufiyaa	Dhivehi	116
AFRICA						
FLAG	COUNTRY	CAPITAL	POPULATION	CURRENCY	OFFICIAL LANG.	AREA (SQ MILES)
	Sudan	Khartoum	26,700,000	Sudanese dinar	Arabic	967,500
	Algeria	Algiers	26,400,000	Algerian dinar	Arabic	919,590
	Zaire	Kinshasa	39,900,000	New zaire	French	905,560
	Libya	Tripoli	4,900,000	Libyan dinar	Arabic	679,360
	Chad	N'Djamena	5,800,000	CFA franc	French	495,750

Flag	Country	Capital	Population	Currency	Official lang.	Area (sq miles)
	Niger	Niamey	8,300,000	CFA franc	French	489,190
	Angola	Luanda	9,900,000	New kwanza	Portuguese	481,350
	Mali	Bamako	9,800,000	CFA franc	French	478,840
	Ethiopia	Addis Ababa	53,000,000	Ethiopian birr	Amharic	471,780
	South Africa	Pretoria, Cape Town, Bloemfontein	37,400,000	Rand	11 African languages, English, Afrikaans	471,440
	Mauritania	Nouakchott	2,100,000	Ouguiya	French	395,950
	Egypt	Cairo	54,800,000	Egyptian pound	Arabic	386,660
	Tanzania	Dodoma	27,800,000	Tanzanian shilling	English, Swahili	364,900
	Nigeria	Abuja	90,000,000	Naira	English	356,670
	Namibia	Windhoek	1,500,000	South African rand	English	318,260
	Mozambique	Maputo	16,100,000	Metical	Portuguese	309,490
	Zambia	Lusaka	8,600,000	Zambian kwacha	English, Bemba, Nyanja	290,560
	Somalia	Mogadishu	9,200,000	Somali shilling	Somali, Arabic	246,200
	Central African Republic	Bangui	3,200,000	CFA franc	French	240,530
	Madagascar	Antananarivo	11,900,000	Malagasy franc	Malagasy, French	226,660
	Botswana	Gaborone	1,300,000	Pula	English	224,600
	Kenya	Nairobi	25,200,000	Kenya shilling	Swahili	224,080
	Cameroon	Yaoundé	12,200,000	CFA franc	French, English	183,570
	Morocco (+W. Sahara)	Rabat	26,300,000	Moroccan dirham	Arabic	172,420 (+97,340)
	Zimbabwe	Harare	10,600,000	Zimbabwe dollar	English	150,800
	Congo	Brazzaville	2,400,000	CFA franc	French	132,040

Flag	Country	Capital	Population	Currency	Official lang.	Area (sq miles)
	Ivory Coast	Yamoussoukro	12,900,000	CFA franc	French	124,500
	Burkina	Ouagadougou	9,500,000	CFA franc	French	105,870
	Gabon	Libreville	1,200,000	CFA franc	French	103,350
	Guinea	Conakry	5,900,000	Guinea franc	French	94,930
	Ghana	Accra	16,000,000	Cedi	English	92,100
	Uganda	Kampala	18,700,000	New Uganda shilling	English	91,070
	Senegal	Dakar	7,700,000	CFA franc	French	75,950
	Tunisia	Tunis	8,400,000	Tunisian dinar	Arabic	63,170
	Malawi	Lilongwe	10,400,000	Malawian kwacha	Chewa, English	45,750
	Benin	Porto-Novo	4,900,000	CFA franc	French	43,480
	Liberia	Monrovia	2,800,000	Liberian dollar	English	43,000
	Eritrea	Asmara	3,500,000	Egyptian pound	Tigrinya, Arabic	36,170
	Sierra Leone	Freetown	4,400,000	Leone	English	27,700
	Togo	Lomé	3,800,000	CFA franc	French, Kabye, Ewe	21,930
	Guinea-Bissau	Bissau	1,000,000	Guinea peso	Portuguese	13,940
	Lesotho	Maseru	1,800,000	Loti	English, Sesotho	11,720
	Equatorial Guinea	Malabo	400,000	CFA franc	Spanish	10,830
	Burundi	Bujumbura	5,800,000	Burundi franc	French, Kirundi	10,750
	Rwanda	Kigali	7,400,000	Rwanda franc	French, Kinyarwanda	10,170
	Djibouti	Djibouti	500,000	Djibouti franc	Arabic, French	8,960
	Swaziland	Mbabane	800,000	Lilangeni	Siswati, English	6,700

FLAG	COUNTRY	CAPITAL	POPULATION	CURRENCY	OFFICIAL LANG.	AREA (SQ MILES)
	The Gambia	Banjul	900,000	Dalasi	English	4,360
	Cape Verde	Cidade de Praia	400,000	Cape Verde escudo	Portuguese	1,560
	Comoros	Moroni	600,000	Comoros franc	Arabic, French	861
	Mauritius	Port Louis	1,100,000	Mauritian rupee	English	718
	São Tomé & Principe	São Tomé	124,000	Dobra	Portuguese	372
	Seychelles	Victoria	68,000	Seychelles rupee	Creole	108

AUSTRALASIA						
FLAG	COUNTRY	CAPITAL	POPULATION	CURRENCY	OFFICIAL LANG.	AREA (SQ MILES)
	Australia	Canberra	17,600,000	Australian dollar	English	2,967,890
	Papua New Guinea	Port Moresby	4,100,000	Kina	Pidgin English, Motu	178,700
	New Zealand	Wellington	3,500,000	New Zealand dollar	English	103,730
	Solomon Islands	Honiara	300,000	Solomon Islands dollar	English	111,580
	Fiji	Suva	700,000	Fiji dollar	English	7,050
	Vanuatu	Port-Vila	163,000	Vatu	Bislama, English, French	4,710
	Micronesia	Kolonia	101,000	US dollar	English	1,120
	Western Samoa	Apia	169,000	Tala	Samoan, English	1,100
	Tonga	Nuku'alofa	94,000	Pa'anga	Tongan	290
	Kiribati	Bairiki	73,000	Australian dollar	English	274
	Palau	Koror	16,400	US dollar	Palauan, English	178
	Marshall Islands	Majuro	48,000	US dollar	English, Marshallese	70
	Tuvalu	Funafuti	9,061	Australian dollar, Tuvaluan dollar	None	10
	Nauru	None	9,400	Australian dollar	Nauruan	8.2

AMERICAN STATES

THE UNITED STATES OF AMERICA is made up of 50 states and the District of Columbia (also known as Washington, DC). The two most recently enlisted states, Alaska and Hawaii (both 1959), are separate from the main landmass.

ALASKA
Alaska, the largest in area, is the least populated state. In 1867, the US bought Alaska from Russia for only $7.2 million. Today, great deposits of oil and natural gas, found in 1968, are mined.

HAWAII
Consisting of a group of about 130 Pacific islands, Hawaii is 2,090 miles from the continental US. It is the most recent state of the US, and is best known for its volcanic activity.

THE WHITE HOUSE
The White House in
Washington, DC, is the
official residence of the
President and his family.
Designed by James
Hoban, it was destroyed
by British troops in 1814
and then rebuilt.

UNITED STATES

400 km

400 miles

C A N A D A

NORTH
DAKOTA
• Bismark

MINNESOTA

MAINE

VERM. • Augusta

St. Paul •

Montpelier NEW HAM.

NEW YORK Concord

SOUTH
DAKOTA
• Pierre

WISCONSIN

Albany • MASS. • Boston
Providence
Hartford • RHODE IS.
CONN.

NEBRASKA

IOWA

Madison •

MICHIGAN

Lansing •

Des Moines •

PENNSYLVANIA NEW JERSEY

INDIANA OHIO Harrisburg •

Lincoln •

Trenton

Springfield

Columbus WEST MARYLAND DELAWARE
VIRGINIA

nver

Topeka •

ILLINOIS Indianapolis •

Charleston

KANSAS

Jefferson
City •

MISSOURI

Frankfort •

KENTUCKY

VIRGINIA

Richmond

NORTH

Raleigh

• Nashville

CAROLINA

OKLAHOMA
City •

ARKANSAS

TENNESSEE

Columbia

OKLAHOMA

Little Rock •

ALABAMA

Atlanta • SOUTH
CAROLINA

T E X A S

MISSISSIPPI

GEORGIA

N

Jackson • Montgomery

LOUISIANA

• Tallahassee

• Austin

Baton
Rouge

F L O R I D A

COAL

WORLD RESOURCES

THE BASIC RAW MATERIALS for living all come from the Earth. Some are renewable resources, like cultivated foods, while others, such as fossil fuels, are nonrenewable. As the global population increases, so humankind draws relentlessly on the Earth. This has led to wasteful exploitation of resources in order to satisfy modern "needs."

COAL

The table shows the world's top producers per annum.

COUNTRY	TONS
China	1,230,588,000
US	997,547,000
Germany	504,971,000
Russia	346,082,000
India	280,689,000

CRUDE OIL

The table shows production in barrels per annum.

COUNTRY	BARRELS P.A.
Saudi Arabia	2,979,000,000
Russia	65,374,000
US	56,762,000
Iran	42,480,000
China	29,324,000

ELECTRICITY

The table shows production annually in kilowatt hours.

COUNTRY	KW/HR
US	3,074,504,000,000
Russia	904,959,000
Japan	458,102,000
China	313,960,000
Germany	254,600,000

LEADING PRODUCERS OF MINERALS

MATERIAL	TOP PRODUCERS	TOTAL* (in millions)	WORLD TOTAL* (in millions)
Bauxite	Australia	41.2	
	Guinea	18.2	1,173
Coal	China	1,162	
	US	980	6,484
Copper	Chile	1.8	
	US	1.7	10.1
Natural gas	CIS (prev. USSR)	28,110 cu ft	
	US	17,262 cu ft	74,160,870 cu ft
Iron ore	CIS	288	
	China	182	1,085
Kaolin (clay)	CIS	2.2	
	Republic of Korea	1.4	25.4
Salt	US	39.1	
	China	31.2	
Sulfur	US	12.8	
	China	8.1	66.5

*All figures in tons apart from cu ft = cubic feet.

WHEAT

These tables show the top producers of staple crops.

COUNTRY	TONS
China	115,748,000
US	72,063,000
India	65,569,000
Russia	46,826,000
France	32,324,000
Canada	30,672,000

RICE

Rice is the only crop that can support Asia's population.

COUNTRY	TONS
China	206,365,000
India	122,369,000
Indonesia	52,782,000
Bangladesh	30,864,000
Vietnam	24,582,000
Thailand	21,043,000

CORN

First grown in the Americas, corn is a prime cereal crop.

COUNTRY	TONS
US	177,632,000
China	113,957,000
Brazil	33,032,000
Mexico	20,503,000
France	16,497,000
Argentina	12,012,000

LEADING AGRICULTURAL PRODUCERS

Today, farming and fishing are major international businesses, with countries competing in the export market. This table shows where products are derived by listing the top three producers of wide-ranging agricultural products.

PRODUCT	TOP PRODUCER	SECOND	THIRD
Cattle	Australia	Brazil	US
Coffee	Brazil	Colombia	Indonesia
Cotton	China	US	CIS
Cow's milk	US	Germany	Russia
Hen's eggs	China	US	Russia
Hogs	China	US	Russia
Corn	US	China	Brazil
Oats	CIS	US	Canada
Potatoes	Russia	Poland	China
Rice	China	India	Indonesia
Rubber	Malaysia	Indonesia	Thailand
Sheep	Australia	China	New Zealand
Soy beans	US	Brazil	China
Tea	India	China	Sri Lanka
Tobacco	China	US	India
Wheat	China	US	India
Wood	US	Russia	China
Wool	Australia	CIS	New Zealand

FISH CATCHES

This table gives fish catches per year in the given area.

AREA	TONS*
Pacific Ocean	53.26
Atlantic Ocean	22.23
Indian Ocean	6.54
Mediterranean and Black Sea	1.42
Antarctic	0.44
World total	83.90

*catch in million metric tons (1989–91)

FISHING IN THE NORTH SEA

US PRESIDENTS

WITH THE END of the Cold War in the 1990s, the President of the US became the most powerful leader in the world. Presidents are elected to serve a 4-year term of office. Since 1951, no president is permitted to serve more than two terms.

LINCOLN MEMORIAL, WASHINGTON, DC.

PRESIDENTS OF THE US			
1789–97	George Washington	1885–89	Grover S. Cleveland
1797–1801	John Adams	1889–93	Benjamin Harrison
1801–09	Thomas Jefferson	1893–97	Grover S. Cleveland
1809–17	James Madison	1897–1901	William McKinley
1817–25	James Monroe	1901–09	Theodore Roosevelt
1825–29	John Quincy Adams	1909–13	William H. Taft
1829–37	Andrew Jackson	1913–21	Woodrow Wilson
1837–41	Martin van Buren	1921–23	Warren G. Harding
1841	William H. Harrison	1923–29	Calvin Coolidge
1841–45	John Tyler	1929–33	Herbert Hoover
1845–49	James K. Polk	1933–45	Franklin D. Roosevelt
1849–50	Zachary Taylor	1945–53	Harry S. Truman
1850–53	Millard Fillmore	1953–61	Dwight D. Eisenhower
1853–57	Franklin Pierce	1961–63	John F. Kennedy
1857–61	James Buchanan	1963–69	Lyndon B. Johnson
1861–65	Abraham Lincoln	1969–74	Richard Nixon
1865–69	Andrew Johnson	1974–77	Gerald Ford
1869–77	Ulysses S. Grant	1977–81	James Carter
1877–81	Rutherford B. Hayes	1981–89	Ronald Reagan
1881	James A. Garfield	1989–93	George Bush
1881–85	Chester A. Arthur	1993–	William J. Clinton

RUSSIAN RULERS

FOR MOST OF ITS HISTORY, Russia was a monarchy in which the Czar or Czarina held absolute power. The 1917 Bolshevik Revolution changed the style of politics, as did the fall of Communism in 1992. Today, supreme power lies with an elected president.

RUSSIAN MONARCHS			
1462–1505	Ivan III, the Great	1725–27	Catherine I
1505–33	Basil III	1727–30	Peter II
1533–84	Ivan IV, the Terrible	1730–40	Anna
1584–98	Fyodor I	1740–41	Ivan VI
1598–1605	Boris Gudunov	1741–62	Elizabeth
1605	Fyodor II	1762	Peter III
1605–06	Demetrius	1762–96	Catherine II, the Great
1606–10	Basil (IV) Shuiski	1796–1801	Paul I
1610–13	Interregnum (interval in reigns)	1801–25	Alexander I
1613–45	Michael Romanov	1825–55	Nicholas I
1645–76	Alexis	1855–81	Alexander II
1676–82	Fyodor III	1881–94	Alexander III
1682–89	Ivan V and Peter I, the Great	1894–1917	Nicholas II
1689–1725	Peter I, the Great	1917	Bolshevik Revolution

LEADERS OF THE USSR		
	1917–22	Vladimir Lenin
	1922–53	Joseph Stalin
	1953–64	Nikita Krushchev
	1964–82	Leonid Brezhnev
	1982–84	Yuri Andropov
	1984–85	Konstantin Chernenko
	1985–92	Mikhail Gorbachev
JOSEPH STALIN	1992–	Boris Yeltsin

JOSEPH STALIN

SPASSKY TOWER
This is the most impressive tower in the Kremlin, Moscow's ruling center.

British rulers

These lists detail the monarchs of England and Scotland up to the early 17th century and, following the unification of England and Scotland, the joint British monarchs up to the present day.

ELIZABETH I

MONARCHS OF ENGLAND

SAXON

1042–66	Edward the Confessor
1066	Harold II

NORMAN

1066–87	William I, the Conqueror
1087–1100	William II
1100–35	Henry I
1135–54	Stephen

PLANTAGENET

1154–89	Henry II
1189–99	Richard I, the Lionheart
1199–1216	John
1216–72	Henry III
1272–1307	Edward I
1307–27	Edward II
1327–77	Edward III
1377–99	Richard II

LANCASTER

1399–1413	Henry IV
1413–22	Henry V
1422–61	Henry VI

YORK

1461–83	Edward IV
1483	Edward V
1483–85	Richard III

TUDOR

1485–1509	Henry VII
1509–47	Henry VIII
1547–53	Edward VI
1553–58	Mary I
1558–1603	Elizabeth I

MONARCHS OF SCOTLAND

1306–29	Robert I, the Bruce
1329–71	David II

STUART

1371–90	Robert II
1390–1406	Robert III
1406–37	James I
1437–60	James II
1460–88	James III
1488–1513	James IV
1513–42	James V
1542–67	Mary, Queen of Scots
1567–1625	James VI

MONARCHS OF BRITAIN

STUART

1603–25	James I (VI of Scotland)
1625–49	Charles I
1649–60	Commonwealth

STUART

1660–85	Charles II
1685–88	James II
1689–94	Mary II
1689–1702	William III
1702–14	Anne

HANOVER

1714–27	George I
1727–60	George II
1760–1820	George III
1820–30	George IV
1830–37	William IV
1837–1901	Victoria

SAXE-COBURG

1901–10	Edward VII

WINDSOR

1910–36	George V
1936	Edward VIII
1936–52	George VI
1952–	Elizabeth II

BRITISH PRIME MINISTERS

1721–42	Robert Walpole
1742–43	Earl of Wilmington
1743–54	Henry Pelham
1754–56	Duke of Newcastle
1756–57	Duke of Devonshire
1757–62	Duke of Newcastle
1762–63	Earl of Bute
1763–65	George Grenville
1765–66	Marquess of Rockingham
1766–68	Earl of Chatham, Pitt the Elder
1768–70	Duke of Grafton
1770–82	Lord North
1782	Marquess of Rockingham
1782–83	Earl of Shelburne
1783	Duke of Portland
1783–1801	William Pitt, the Younger
1801–04	Henry Addington
1804–06	William Pitt, the Younger
1806–07	Lord Grenville
1807–09	Duke of Portland
1809–12	Spencer Perceval
1812–27	Earl of Liverpool
1827	George Canning
1827–28	Viscount Goderich
1828–30	Duke of Wellington
1830–34	Earl Grey
1834	Viscount Melbourne
1834–35	Robert Peel
1835–41	Viscount Melbourne
1841–46	Robert Peel
1846–52	Lord John Russell
1852	Earl of Derby
1852–55	Earl of Aberdeen
1855–58	Viscount Palmerston
1858–59	Earl of Derby
1859–65	Viscount Palmerston
1865–66	Earl Russell
1866–68	Earl of Derby
1868	Benjamin Disraeli
1868–74	William Gladstone
1874–80	Benjamin Disraeli
1880–85	William Gladstone
1885–86	Marquess of Salisbury
1886	William Gladstone
1886–92	Marquess of Salisbury
1892–94	William Gladstone
1894–95	Earl of Rosebery
1895–1902	Marquess of Salisbury
1902–05	Arthur Balfour
1905–08	Henry Campbell-Bannerman
1908–16	Herbert Asquith
1916–22	David Lloyd George
1922–23	Andrew Bonar Law
1923–24	Stanley Baldwin
1924	James Ramsay MacDonald
1924–29	Stanley Baldwin
1929–35	James Ramsay MacDonald
1935–37	Stanley Baldwin
1937–40	Neville Chamberlain
1940–45	Winston Churchill
1945–51	Clement Attlee
1951–55	Winston Churchill
1955–57	Anthony Eden
1957–63	Harold Macmillan
1963–64	Sir Alec Douglas-Home
1964–70	Harold Wilson
1970–74	Edward Heath
1974–76	Harold Wilson
1976–79	James Callaghan
1979–90	Margaret Thatcher
1990–	John Major

Ancient rulers and dynasties

Throughout history, many civilizations have endured over long periods of time. The ancient Egyptians established an extremely advanced society, consolidating ruling power around the cult of the pharaoh. The Chinese passed on their culture in the form of succeeding dynasties. The Japanese characterized their history through succeeding periods that colored political, military, and cultural life. The Catholic Church has maintained its inheritance through a lineage of popes that extends directly from St Peter.

OSIRIS, EGYPTIAN GOD OF THE UNDERWORLD

EGYPTIAN PERIODS		
PERIOD	DATE	MAIN PHARAOH
Early dynastic	c.3100–c.2686 BC	Narmer (Menes)
Old Kingdom	c.2686–c.2160 BC	Zoser
		Khufu
First Intermediate Period	c.2160–c.2130 BC	
Middle Kingdom	c.2130–c.1786 BC	Mentuhotep II
Second Intermediate Period	c.1786–c.1550 BC	Hyksos rule
New Kingdom	c.1550–c.1050 BC	Amenhotep I
		Queen Hatshepsut
		Thutmose III
		Akhenaton
		Tutankhamun
		Rameses II
Third Intermediate Period	c.1050–667 BC	Nubian rule
Early dynastic	c.664–333 BC	Darius III
Early dynastic	333–30 BC	Alexander the Great
		Ptolemy I Soter
		Queen Cleopatra VII

Key Roman Rulers

Roman Republic (Rulers)	Reign
Lucius Cornelius Sulla	82–78 BC
Pompey, Crassus, Caesar (First Triumvirate)	60–53 BC
Pompey	52–47 BC
Julius Caesar	46–44 BC
Mark Antony, Octavian, Lepidus (Second Triumvirate)	43–31 BC
Roman empire (Emperors)	Reign
Augustus (Octavian)	27 BC– AD 14
Tiberius	14–37
Caligula	37–41
Claudius	41–54
Nero	54–68
Vespasian	69–79
Titus	79–81
Domitian	81–96
Trajan	98–117

Chinese Dynasties and Republics

Dynasty	Dates (AD)
Three Kingdoms	220–265
Western Chin	265–317
Eastern Chin	317–420
Southern	420–589
Sui	589–618
T'ang	618–690
Chou	690–705
T'ang	705–907
Northern Five, Southern Ten	907–960
Song (Sung)	960–1279
Yuan (Mongol)	1279–1368
Ming	1368–1644
Qing (Manchu)	1644–1911
Republic (Nationalist)	1911–1949
People's Republic (Communist)	1949–

Japanese Periods*

Period	Date (AD)	
Yamato	250–710	
Nara	710–794	
Heian	794–1192	
Kamakura	1192–1333	
Muromachi	1333–1573	
Momoyama	1573–1603	
Edo	1603–1867	
Meiji	1867–1912	
Taisho	1912–1926	Japanese
Showa	1926–1989	Warlord
Heisei	1989–	

*Japanese historical periods began with political unity and the introduction of an emperor figure.

Key Popes

Pope	Reign (AD)	
St Peter	c.42–67	
St Clement I	c.88–97	
St Stephen I	254–257	
St Leo I, the Great	440–461	
St Gregory I, the Great	590–604	
St Leo IX	1049–54	
St Gregory VII	1073–85	
Urban II	1088–99	
Innocent III	1198–1216	
Alexander VI	1492–1503	
Paul III	1534–49	
Gregory XIII	1572–85	
Pius IX	1846–78	
John XXIII	1958–63	Rosary
John Paul II	1978–	Beads

MAJOR WARS

IN THE PAST, wars were decided by armies on battlefields. Today, technology has vastly increased modern warfare's destructive power.

GATLING GUN

MAJOR WARS AND REVOLUTIONS			
DATE	CONFLICT	VICTOR(S)	LOSER(S)
c.1096–1291	Crusades	Muslims	European Christians
c.1137–1453	Hundred Years War	France	England
1455–85	Wars of the Roses	House of Lancaster	House of York
1618–48	Thirty Years War	European Protestants	European Catholics
1642–49	English Civil War	Parliamentarians	Royalists
1701–13	War of the Spanish Succession	Austria	France
1756–63	Seven Years War	Britain, Hanover, Prussia	Austria, France, Russia, Sweden
1775–83	American Revolution	American colonies	Britain
1789	French Revolution	Jacobins	Royalists
1792–1815	Napoleonic Wars	Austria, Britain, Russia, Prussia, Sweden	France
1812–14	War of 1812	US	Britain
1846–48	Mexican–American War	US	Mexico
1853–56	Crimean War	Britain, France, Sardinia, Turkey	Russia
1861–65	American Civil War	Unionists	Confederates
1870–71	Franco–Prussian War	Prussia	France
1899–1902	Boer War	British Commonwealth	Boers
1904–05	Russo–Japanese War	Japan	Russia

GERMAN SWEPT-HILT RAPIER

DATE	CONFLICT	VICTOR(S)	LOSER(S)
1917	Russian Revolution	Bolsheviks	Royalists
1914–18	World War I	British Commonwealth, Belgium, France, Italy, Russia, US	Germany, Austria-Hungary, Turkey
1936–39	Spanish Civil War	Nationalists	Republicans
1937–45	Chinese–Japanese War	China	Japan
1939–45	World War II	British Commonwealth, USSR, US	Germany, Italy, Japan
1945-49	Chinese Revolution	Communists	Nationalists
1950–53	Korean War	South Korea, UN	North Korea
1957–75	Vietnam War	North Vietnam	South Vietnam, US and allies
1967	Six-Day War	Israel	Egypt
1967–70	Nigerian Civil War	Federalists	Biafrans
1973	October War	Israel	Arab nations
1980–88	Iran–Iraq War	negotiated ceasefire	
1991	Gulf War	US-led coalition	Iraq
1991–95	Bosnian Civil War	negotiated ceasefire	

NAZI STANDARD BEARER

KEY BATTLES			
DATE	NAME	VICTOR(S)	LOSER(S)
1066	Hastings (England)	Normans	Saxons
1415	Agincourt (France)	England	France
1588	Spanish Armada (England)	England	Spain
1805	Trafalgar	Britain	France, Spain
1805	Austerlitz (Czech Republic)	France	Austria, Russia
1815	Waterloo (Belgium)	Britain, Holland, Belgium, Prussia	France
1863	Gettysburg (US)	Unionists	Confederates
1916	The Somme (France)	British Commonwealth	Germany
1942	Midway (Pacific)	US	Japan
1943	Stalingrad (Russia)	USSR	Germany
1944	Normandy (France)	US, British Commonwealth	Germany

WAR FACTS

• War this century has killed 100 million people; 20 million since 1945.

• In World War I, about 19 million died: 95% soldiers, 5% civilians.

• In World War II, more than 50 million died: 50% soldiers, 50% civilians.

• Over 150 wars have broken out since 1945.

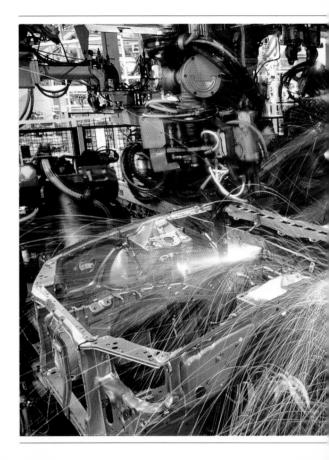

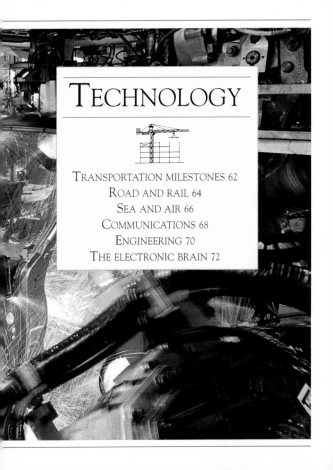

TECHNOLOGY

TRANSPORTATION MILESTONES

THROUGHOUT HISTORY, people have always desired to move as quickly and freely as possible. Human ingenuity has led to countless transportation inventions, from the wheel to the jet engine.

8000 BC – AD 1119	1522 – 1815	1829 – 1881
• 8000 BC First long-distance sea voyage, from the Greek mainland to the island of Melos. • 4500 BC Europe, Turkey, Iran: horses tamed for the first time. • 3500 BC Wheeled vehicles in use in Mesopotamia. *875–985 VIKING LONGSHIP* • 1900 BC First long-distance roads in Europe. • 605 Work completed on China's Grand Canal, which runs over 600 miles (1000 km). • 875–985 Viking ships dominate the seas of northern Europe. • 1119 Early form of compass used by Chinese as navigation aid.	• 1522 Portuguese Ferdinand Magellan, in his ship the *Vittoria*, is the first person to sail around the world. • c.1700 Introduction of ship's steering wheel. • 1776 A one-person submarine, the *Turtle*, designed by American David C. Bushnell, is used in an attack on a British warship. *c.1700 SHIP'S WHEEL* • 1783 French brothers Joseph and Étienne Montgolfier launch a hot-air balloon from Versailles, France. • 1804 First successful steam locomotive built, by Englishman Richard Trevithick. • 1815 Scotsman John L. McAdam develops macadam road-making material.	• 1829 The *Rocket*, built by Englishman George Stephenson, ushers in the age of rail travel. • 1830 UK: First public steam railroad, called the Liverpool & Manchester. • 1835 Invention of the screw propeller. • 1839 Invention of the pedal-driven bicycle. • 1852 Frenchman Henri Giffard builds and flies the first airship. • 1869 Opening of the Suez Canal in Egypt. • 1881 The world's first electric railroad opens in Germany. *1852 GIFFARD'S AIRSHIP*

| 1886 – 1913 | 1914 – 1955 | 1961 – 1994 |

- 1886 Gottlieb Daimler makes prototype car by fixing an engine to a horse-drawn carriage.
- 1890 UK: Opening of the first underground railroad, the City and South London line.
- 1892 First commercially produced motorbike.
- 1892 German Rudolph Diesel develops the diesel engine.
- 1895 Germany's Kiel ship canal is completed.
- 1903 American Orville Wright makes the

1913
MODEL T FORD

first successful flight in the *Flyer*.
- 1907 Frenchman Paul Cornu makes the first helicopter flight.
- 1909 Frenchman Louis Blériot is first to fly the English Channel.
- 1913 American Henry Ford's Model T is the first mass-produced car.

- 1914 Panama Canal opens.

1939 HEINKEL HE 178

- 1919 First nonstop flight across the Atlantic by British aviators John Alcock and Arthur Whitten-Brown.
- 1926 Launch of the first liquid-fueled rocket, designed by American Robert Goddard.
- 1937 British engineer Frank Whittle designs the jet engine.
- 1938 UK: The *Mallard* sets a world speed record for steam traction of 126 mph (203 km/h).
- 1939 The German Heinkel HE 178 makes the first jet-propelled flight.
- 1947 American test pilot Chuck Yeager breaks the sound barrier in a rocket-powered plane, the *Bell X-1*.
- 1952 The world's first jet airliner, the De Havilland Comet, enters service.
- 1955 US: Launch of the first nuclear submarine, the *Nautilus*.

- 1961 Russian Yuri Gagarin is the first person in space, in *Vostok I*.
- 1969 American astronauts Neil Armstrong and "Buzz" Aldrin land on the Moon, in *Apollo II*.
- 1970 The Boeing 747 "Jumbo Jet" comes into commercial service.
- 1979 A human-powered aircraft, the *Gossamer Albatross*, crosses the English Channel.
- 1981 A reusable spacecraft, US shuttle *Colombia*, is launched.
- 1986 The *Rutan Voyager* makes the first nonstop, round-the-world flight.
- 1990 France: a TGV electric train sets a world rail speed record of 320 mph (515 km/h).
- 1994 Opening of the Channel Tunnel rail link between France and England.

1990 TGV TRAIN

ROAD AND RAIL

THE MOTOR VEHICLE AND TRAIN are the main forms of land transportation. This century has witnessed increasing roadroad and highway networks that try to service burgeoning populations and economic growth. Pollution from motor vehicles is now a serious threat to the environment.

ROAD HAULAGE

Most goods are carried by motor vehicles since highways can carry more traffic than railroads. This table lists those countries that transport the most goods a year by road.

COUNTRY	GOODS TRANSPORTED (TONS)
US	1,312,000,000
China	375,000,000
Russia	331,000,000
Japan	309,000,000
Brazil	298,000,000
India	243,000,000

COUNTRIES WITH THE MOST ROADS

COUNTRY	MILES (KM)
US	3,879,284 (6,243,103)
India	1,224,101 (1,970,000)
Brazil	1,037,782 (1,670,000)
Japan	938,736 (1,510,750)
China	693,207 (1,115,609)

TOP VEHICLE-OWNING COUNTRIES IN THE WORLD

COUNTRY	CARS	COMMERCIAL VEHICLES	TOTAL
US	144,213,429	46,148,799	190,362,228
Japan	38,963,793	22,694,351	61,658,144
Germany	39,086,000	2,923,000	42,009,000
Italy	29,497,000	2,763,000	32,260,050
France	24,020,000	5,040,000	26,651,740

TOP VEHICLE-PRODUCING COUNTRIES

COUNTRY	CARS	COMMERCIAL VEHICLES	TOTAL
Japan	8,497,094	2,730,451	11,237,545
US	5,981,046	4,883,157	10,864,203
Germany	3,753,341	237,309	3,990,650
France	2,836,280	319,437	3,155,717
Canada	1,349,081	888,652	2,237,733

TRAFFIC JAMS
On average, car drivers spend 5.4 days per year in traffic jams

EUROSTAR
Following the construction of the
Channel Tunnel, a new train was
specially designed to be used on this
network. Known as
"Eurostar," it can travel at
a maximum speed of
186 mph (300 km/h).

LONGEST SUBWAYS		
CITY	STATIONS	MILES (KM)
Washington, DC	86	380 (612)
London	272	267 (430)
New York	461	230 (370)
Paris (Metro & RER)	430	187 (301)
Moscow	115	140 (225)

RAILS
Rail lines are
laid as a pair of
continuous and
parallel steel tracks,
along which trains
can run smoothly.

Switches
allow trains
to change
direction

Wooden
sleepers
suppport
steel tracks

LONGEST RAILROAD TUNNELS			
TUNNEL	COUNTRY	DATE BUILT	LENGTH MILES (KM)
Alp Transit Link	Switzerland	2007	35.4 (57)
Seikan	Japan	1985	33.5 (53.9)
Channel	France/ UK	1994	32.2 (51.8)
Northern line	UK	1939	17.3 (27.8)
Daishimizu	Japan	1982	13.8 (22.2)

COUNTRES WITH THE MOST TRACK	
COUNTRY	TOTAL MILES (KM) OF TRACK
US	149,129 (240,000)
Russia	98,239 (158,100)
Canada	90,996 (146,444)
China	39,768 (64,000)
India	38,432 (61,850)
Germany	28,253 (45,468)
Australia	25,152 (40,478)
France	21,327 (34,322)
Argentina	21,223 (34,172)
Brazil	18,724 (30,133)

TILTING TRAIN
The Italian ETR
450 tilts at an
angle of up to 10°.

TRANSPORT FACTS
• At 15,705 ft, Condor,
Bolivia is the world's
highest railroad station.

• More than 130,000
steam locomotives were
built in Britain from
1804–1968.

• General Motors
produces over 5.5
million cars a year.

SEA AND AIR

AS TECHNOLOGY increases communication around the world, so the ability to travel becomes more common. Today, shipping transports about 90 percent of international goods, aided by ship canals that provide shorter global routes. Airlines offer faster passenger services to worldwide destinations, carrying millions of people daily.

HEATHROW AIRPORT
The busiest international airport in the world caters to over 40 million people each year. Business benefits the most from increased air travel, and many use Heathrow as a meeting point on connecting flights.

BUSIEST INTERNATIONAL AIRPORTS IN THE WORLD	
AIRPORT	INTERNATIONAL PASSENGERS PER ANNUM
London Heathrow, UK	40,844,000
Frankfurt, Germany	25,195,000
Hong Kong	24,421,000
Charles de Gaulle, France	22,336,000
Schipol, Netherlands	20,659,000
Tokyo/Narita, Japan	18,947,000
Singapore International	18,796,000
London Gatwick, UK	18,660,000
JFK International, US	15,014,000
Bangkok, Thailand	12,755,000

AIRLINE PASSENGER TRAFFIC 1995	
AIRLINE	PASSENGERS (MILLIONS)
Alitalia Italian Airlines	20.0
American Airlines	80.0
British Airways	30.0
Delta Airlines	87.0
Emirates Airways	3.0
Gulf Air	5.0
JAL (Japan Air)	32.7
KLM (Royal Dutch Air)	11.2
Lufthansa (German Airlines)	40.7
Singapore Air	10.7
Virgin Atlantic Airways	2.0

MAJOR PORTS	
PORT (COUNTRY)	TOTAL GOODS HANDLED (TONS)
Rotterdam (Netherlands)	318,000,000
New Orleans (US)	209,000,000
Singapore (Singapore)	207,000,000
Kobe (Japan)	190,000,000
Shanghai (China)	147,000,000
Houston (US)	144,000,000

AIR AND SEA FACTS

• The world's largest ship, the tanker *Jahre Viking*, is 1,503 ft long.

• The Boeing 747-700, the largest airliner, has a wingspan of 211 ft.

COUNTRIES WITH HIGHEST TONNAGE		
COUNTRY OF SHIPS	NUMBER	TOTAL GRT*
Panama	5,564	57,618,623
Liberia	1,611	53,918,534
Greece	1,929	29,134,435
Japan	9,950	24,247,525
Cyprus	1,591	22,842,009
Bahamas	1,121	21,224,164
Norway	785	19,383,417
Russia	5,335	16,813,761
China	2,501	14,944,999
Malta	1,037	14,163,357

* GRT or Gross Registered Tonnage is the cubic capacity of a ship (1 ton = 100 cubic ft)

COUNTRIES WITH THE LONGEST INLAND WATERWAY NETWORKS*		
COUNTRY	MILES	KM
China	86,122	138,600
Russia	62,137	100,000
Brazil	31,069	50,000
US**	25,482	41,009
Indonesia	13,409	21,579
Vietnam	11,000	17,702
India	10,054	16,180
Zaire	9,321	15,000
France	9,278	14,932
Colombia	8,886	14,300

* Canals and navigable rivers
** Excluding the Great Lakes

LONGEST SHIP CANALS					
CANAL	LOCATION	DATE BUILT	LENGTH MILES	KM	
Suez	Links the Red Sea with the Mediterranean	1869	108	174	
Kiel	Links the North Sea with the Baltic Sea, Germany	1895	61	99	
Panama	Links the Atlantic Ocean and the Caribbean with the Pacific Ocean	1914	50	81	
Manchester	Links inland UK canal systems	1894	35	57	

THE MANCHESTER SHIP CANAL

COMMUNICATIONS

COMMUNICATION IS a fundamental human concern. At present, the world is being transformed by a technological revolution that will communicate information across all linguistic and cultural barriers.

SAMUEL MORSE

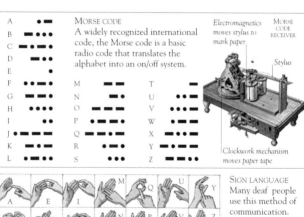

MORSE CODE

A widely recognized international code, the Morse code is a basic radio code that translates the alphabet into an on/off system.

A	●▬	
B	▬●●●	
C	▬●▬●	
D	▬●●	
E	●	
F	●●▬●	
G	▬▬●	
H	●●●●	
I	●●	
J	●▬▬▬	
K	▬●▬	
L	●▬●●	
M	▬▬	
N	▬●	
O	▬▬▬	
P	●▬▬●	
Q	▬▬●▬	
R	●▬●	
S	●●●	
T	▬	
U	●●▬	
V	●●●▬	
W	●▬▬	
X	▬●●▬	
Y	▬●▬▬	
Z	▬▬●●	

Electromagnetics moves stylus to mark paper

MORSE CODE RECEIVER

Stylus

Clockwork mechanism moves paper tape

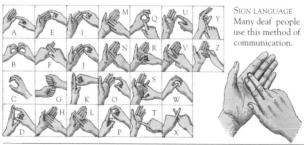

SIGN LANGUAGE

Many deaf people use this method of communication.

A E I M Q U Y
B F J N R V Z
C G K O T W
D H L P S X

SEMAPHORE
This system of signaling with hand-held flags is used as communication between ships at sea.

SATELLITES

Communications satellites that orbit the Earth make contact between countries quicker and easier. Radio waves from the caller are deflected via satellite to a receiver.

GLOBAL INTERNET

Information can now be sent instantly by computers on the growing global network known as the Internet.

W. Asia 0.33%
Oceania 4.41%
S. Asia 0.16%
N. Asia 3.02%
Africa 0.5%
Europe 21.72%
S. America 0.26%
Central America 0.23%
N. America 69.37%

INTERNATIONAL IDENTIFICATION SYSTEM			
A	ALPHA	N	NOVEMBER
B	BRAVO	O	OSCAR
C	CHARLIE	P	PAPA
D	DELTA	Q	QUEBEC
E	ECHO	R	ROMEO
F	FOXTROT	S	SIERRA
G	GOLF	T	TANGO
H	HOTEL	U	UNIFORM
I	INDIA	V	VICTOR
J	JULIET	W	WHISKY
K	KILO	X	X-RAY
L	LIMA	Y	YANKEE
M	MIKE	Z	ZULU

ENGINEERING

HUMANKIND HAS USED construction to improve its
habitat. Buildings are made for housing and to create
working environments; roads, tunnels, and bridges
allow easier movement across the surface of the land;
dams harness nature's power to create electricity.

KEY MODERN ARCHITECTS

NAME	DATES	NATIONALITY	BUILDING
Antonio Gaudi	1852–1926	Spanish	La Sagrada Familia, Barcelona, Spain
Frank Lloyd Wright	1867–1959	American	Guggenheim Museum, New York, US
Walter Gropius	1883–1969	German	Bauhaus, Dessau, Germany
Mies van der Rohe	1886–1969	German	Seagram Building, New York, US
Le Corbusier	1887–1965	Swiss	Nôtre Dame du Haut, Ronchamp, France
Richard Rogers	b.1933	British	Lloyds Building, London, UK

TALLEST BUILDINGS

MASTS AND TOWERS (NOT ILLUSTRATED)	HEIGHT FEET (METERS)
KTHI-TV mast, North Dakota, US	2,064 (629)
KSLA-TV mast, Louisiana, US	1,900 (579)
CN Tower, Toronto, Canada	1,821 (555)

	BUILDING AND LOCATION	HEIGHT FEET (METERS)
1	Petronas Twin Towers, KL, Malaysia	1,483 (452)
2	Sears Tower, Chicago, US	1,453 (443)
3	World Trade Center, New York, US	1,368 (417)
4	Empire State Building, New York, US	1,250 (381)
5	Bank of China, Hong Kong	1,207 (368)
6	Amoco Building, Chicago, US	1,135 (346)
7	John Hancock Center, Chicago, US	1,129 (344)
8	Chrysler Building, New York, US	1,047 (319)
9	Nations Bank Plaza, Atlanta, US	1,024 (312)
10	First Interstate, Los Angeles, US	1,018 (310)

TALLEST DAMS

DAM	LOCATION	DATE BUILT	HEIGHT FEET	METERS
Rogun	Tajikistan	1989	1066	325
Nourek	Tajikistan	1979	1040	317
Grande Dixence	Switzerland	1962	935	285
Inguri	Georgia (CIS)	1979	889	271
Vaiont	Italy	1961	869	265
Mica	British Columbia, Canada	1973	800	244

SUSPENSION BRIDGES WITH LONGEST MAIN SPAN

BRIDGE	COUNTRY	DATE BUILT	LENGTH FEET	METRES
Akashi Kaikyo, Huogo	Japan	1998	6,529	1,990
Great Belt East	Denmark	1997	5,328	1,624
Humber	UK	1981	4,626	1,410
Tsing Ma	Hong Kong	1997	4,518	1,377
Verrazano Narrows	US	1964	4,258	1,298
Golden Gate	US	1937	4,199	1,280
Höga Kusten	Sweden	2000	3,970	1,210
Mackinac Straits	US	1957	3,799	1,158

CIVIL ENGINEERING RECORDS

TITLE	STRUCTURE	SIZE
Longest road	Pan American Highway	1,500 mi
Longest tunnel	New York City / W. Delaware, water supply tunnel, US	105 mi
Longest walled structure	The Great Wall of China	1,460 mi
Largest dome	Louisiana Superdrome, US	679 ft
Deepest mine shaft	Western Deep Levels Gold Mine, South Africa	12,392 ft
Deepest bore hole	Kola Peninsula, Russia	40,682 +ft
Longest oil pipeline	Alberta, Canada/ New York	1,775 mi
Communications cable	ANZCAN telecom. cable	9,414 mi

GOLDEN GATE BRIDGE

FACT BOX

• Over 3,270,000 cu yd of stone was used to construct Egypt's Great Pyramid of Khufu.

• The Pentagon has more than 17 miles (27 km) of corridors.

• The largest shopping centre in the world, West Edmonton Mall, Alberta, Canada, is as big as 90 football fields.

THE ELECTRONIC BRAIN

COMPUTERS SIMPLIFY COMPLEX TASKS into calculations that can be performed quickly. Capable of storing large amounts of information for easy access, they have revolutionized the world of work. Computer performance has so increased, that we are in an age where the electronic brain will soon rival our own.

THE BASIC COMPUTER
Computers are made up of simple, interactive components that allow programs to be run.

Monitor

Microprocessor: carries out a program's instructions

Card systems for extra input

ROM (Read-Only Memory): permanently stored program to make computer ready for use

RAM (Random-Access Memory): stores programs being run

Hard disk

Mouse

Keyboard

TIMELINE

1945 ENIAC (Electronic Numerical Integrator and Calculator) first built in the US.

ENIAC

1948 Manchester Mark I, the first stored-program (RAM) computer is built in the UK. Filling a room the size of a small office, it performs about 500 operations per second.

1958 US engineer Jack Kilby uses semiconductor material to make the first microchip (integrated circuit), using a semiconductor.

MICROCHIP

ARTIFICIAL INTELLIGENCE (AI) Scientists are developing AI to produce thinking computers. The difficulty lies in translating knowledge based on experience and intuition into a mathematical computer logic.

FACT BOX

• The CM-5, the fastest computer, can perfom 131 billion operations per second.

• Computer viruses are programs designed to destroy information in a computer's memory.

• Computers store data in binary: the electrical pulse is either on or off.

COMPUTER LANGUAGES

YEAR	LANGUAGE	MAIN USE	ORIGIN OF NAME
1954	Fortran	Scientific	Formula translator
1956	Lisp	Artificial intelligence	List processor
1959	Cobol	Business	Common businesss oriented language
1960	Algol	Scientific	Algorithimic language
1962	APL	Scientific modeling	A programming language
1964	PL/1	Business	Programming language 1
1965	Basic	Education	Beginner's all-purpose symbolic instruction code
1971	Pascal	Education	Blaise Pascal
1980	Ada	Military, all purpose	Ada Augusta, Lady Lovelace
1995	Visual objects	Database Access	Visual Object oriented program

BINARY CODE

ROMAN	DECIMAL	BINARY	HEX.
I	1	1	1
II	2	10	2
III	3	11	3
IV	4	100	4
V	5	101	5
VI	6	110	6
VII	7	111	7
VIII	8	1000	8
IX	9	1001	9
X	10	1010	A

1964 BASIC (Beginners All-Purpose Symbolic Instruction Code), the popular programming language, is created by professors at Dartmouth College.

1971 Intel 4004, the first microprocessor chip, is produced in the US. It performs 60,000 operations per second. 1977 Mass-produced computers appear.

1990 IBM Pentium PC produced. It can perform 112 million instructions per second.

PERSONAL COMPUTER

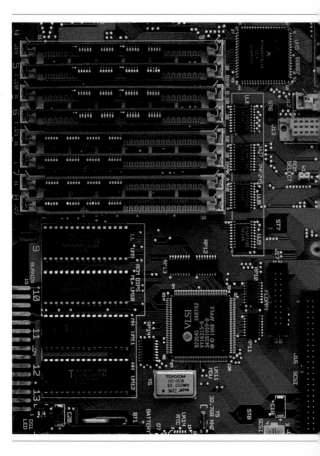

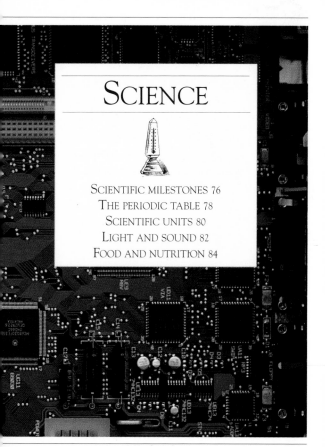

SCIENCE

SCIENTIFIC MILESTONES

FOR CENTURIES, SCIENTISTS have tested their ideas about the physical universe. The discoveries they have made have evolved into a body of knowledge that has revolutionized life on Earth, and led to inventions that have shaped modern civilization.

1620 – 1665	1776 – 1800	1803 – 1833
• 1620s English philosopher Francis Bacon proposes modern scientific method. •1638 Italian scientist Galileo Galilei, the first person to use a telescope, founds mechanics (the study of force and motion). 1638 GALILEO'S TELESCOPE •1661 Irish scientist Robert Boyle realizes nature of chemical elements and compounds. • 1665 English mathematician Isaac Newton formulates the laws of motion and of gravitation. • c.1665 English physicist Robert Hooke develops the microscope.	• 1776 English chemist Henry Cavendish discovers hydrogen. • 1770s French physicist Charles Coulomb studies electrostatic forces. • 1779 French chemist Antoine Lavoisier names oxygen and shows its role in burning. • 1799 Italian chemist Alessandro Volta invents his "voltaic pile" – the world's first battery. • 1800 French physicist André Marie Ampère explores link between electric current and voltage. 1799 VOLTAIC PILE BATTERY	• 1803 Englishman John Dalton proposes modern atomic theory. • 1807–8 British chemist Humphrey Davy discovers potassium, sodium, magnesium, barium, and strontium. • 1811 Italian Amedeo Avogadro formulates law stating that equal volumes of different gases contain the same number of particles. • 1831 English scientist Michael Faraday and American scientist Joseph Henry discover how to use magnetism to create electricity. • 1833 English physicist Michael Faraday discovers the laws of electrolysis. 1833 FARADAY'S RING

1843 – 1896	1897 – 1932	1938 – 1990

- 1843 English scientist James Joule describes relationship between heat, power, and work.
- 1859 Belgian engineer Étienne Lenoir invents the internal combustion engine.

1859 INTERNAL COMBUSTION ENGINE

- 1869 Russian schoolteacher Dmitri Mendeleyev classifies elements into groups by atomic weight, devising the periodic table.
- 1888 German physicist Heinrich Hertz establishes the existence of radio waves.
- 1894 Italian inventor Guglielmo Marconi makes the first radio communication.
- 1895 German physicist Wilhelm Roentgen discovers X rays.
- 1896 French physicist Antoine-Henri Becquerel discovers the effects of radioactivity.

- 1897 British physicist Joseph John Thompson discovers the electron.
- 1898 Polish-French chemists Marie Curie and Pierre Curie isolate radium and polonium.
- 1900 German physicist Max Planck proposes quantum theory.
- 1905 German-born physicist Albert Einstein publishes his *Special Theory of Relativity*.

1905 ALBERT EINSTEIN

- 1909 American chemist Leo Henrick Baekeland invents "Bakelite" plastic.
- 1911 New Zealand-born physicist Ernest Rutherford discovers the atomic nucleus.
- 1931 German physicist Ernst Ruska invents the electron microscope.
- 1932 British physicist James Chadwick discovers the neutron.

- 1938 German scientist Otto Hahn and Austrian physicist Lise Meitner discover nuclear fission.
- 1939 American chemist Linus Pauling explains the chemical bonds between atoms and molecules.
- 1946 American scientist Willard Frank Libby invents the carbon dating process.
- 1960 American physicist Theodore Maiman makes first laser.
- 1964 American physicist Murray Gell-Mann proposes existence of quarks, the smallest particles of matter.
- 1986 Superconductors, substances with very low electrical resistance, are proposed.
- 1990 Satellite discovery of ripples in background radiation supports Big Bang theory of origin of the universe.

1990 THE EXPANDING UNIVERSE

THE PERIODIC TABLE

CERTAIN ELEMENTS SHARE similar chemical properties and atomic structures. These similarities become clear when all the known elements are set out in a chart called the periodic table. This chart arranges elements into "groups"(columns) and "periods"(rows) and atomic structures. As the atomic number increases along each period, the chemical properties of the element gradually change.

1								
1 **H** Hydrogen	**2**							
3 **Li** Lithium	4 **Be** Beryllium							
11 **Na** Sodium	12 **Mg** Magnesium	**3**	**4**	**5**	**6**	**7**	**8**	**9**
19 **K** Potassium	20 **Ca** Calcium	21 **Sc** Scandium	22 **Ti** Titanium	23 **V** Vanadium	24 **Cr** Chromium	25 **Mn** Manganese	26 **Fe** Iron	27 **Co** Cobalt
37 **Rb** Rubidium	38 **Sr** Strontium	39 **Y** Yttrium	40 **Zr** Zirconium	41 **Nb** Niobium	42 **Mo** Molybdenum	43 **Tc** Technetium	44 **Ru** Ruthenium	45 **Rh** Rhodium
55 **Cs** Caesium	56 **Ba** Barium	57–71	72 **Hf** Hafnium	73 **Ta** Tantalum	74 **W** Tungsten	75 **Re** Rhenium	76 **Os** Osmium	77 **Ir** Iridium
87 **Fr** Francium	88 **Ra** Radium	89–103	104 **Unq** Unnil-quadium	105 **Unp** Unnil-pentium	106 **Unh** Unnil-hexium	107 **Uns** Unnil-septium	108 **Uno** Unnil-octium	109 **Une** Unnil-ennium
GROUP I	GROUP II							

Lanthanides and Actinides are separated to give the table a better shape

57 **La** Lanthanum	58 **Ce** Cerium	59 **Pr** Praseo-dymium	60 **Nd** Neodymium	61 **Pm** Promethium	62 **Sm** Samarium
89 **Ac** Actinium	90 **Th** Thorium	91 **Pa** Protact-inium	92 **U** Uranium	93 **Np** Neptunium	94 **Pu** Plutonium

Atomic number

Chemical symbol

15 **P** Phosphorus

Name of element

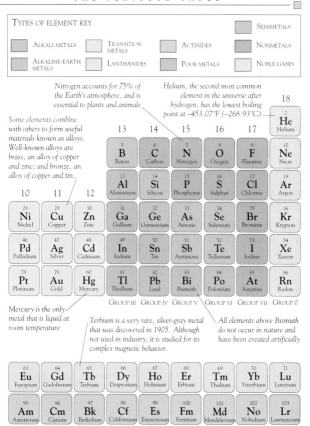

TYPES OF ELEMENT KEY

ALKALI METALS

TRANSITION METALS

ACTINIDES

SEMIMETALS

NONMETALS

ALKALINE-EARTH METALS

LANTHANIDES

POOR METALS

NOBLE GASES

Nitrogen accounts for 75% of the Earth's atmosphere, and is essential to plants and animals

Helium, the second most common element in the universe after hydrogen, has the lowest boiling point at −453.07°F (−268.93°C)

Some elements combine with others to form useful materials known as alloys. Well-known alloys are brass, an alloy of copper and zinc; and bronze, an alloy of copper and tin.

18

2
He
Helium

13 14 15 16 17

5
B
Boron

6
C
Carbon

7
N
Nitrogen

8
O
Oxygen

9
F
Fluorine

10
Ne
Neon

13
Al
Aluminium

14
Si
Silicon

15
P
Phosphorus

16
S
Sulphur

17
Cl
Chlorine

18
Ar
Argon

10 11 12

28
Ni
Nickel

29
Cu
Copper

30
Zn
Zinc

31
Ga
Gallium

32
Ge
Germanium

33
As
Arsenic

34
Se
Selenium

35
Br
Bromine

36
Kr
Krypton

46
Pd
Palladium

47
Ag
Silver

48
Cd
Cadmium

49
In
Indium

50
Sn
Tin

51
Sb
Antimony

52
Te
Tellurium

53
I
Iodine

54
Xe
Xenon

78
Pt
Platinum

79
Au
Gold

80
Hg
Mercury

81
Tl
Thallium

82
Pb
Lead

83
Bi
Bismuth

84
Po
Polonium

85
At
Astatine

86
Rn
Radon

GROUP III GROUP IV GROUP V GROUP VI GROUP VII GROUP 0

Mercury is the only metal that is liquid at room temperature

Terbium is a very rare, silver-gray metal that was discovered in 1905. Although not used in industry, it is studied for its complex magnetic behavior.

All elements above Bismuth do not occur in nature and have been created artificially

63
Eu
Europium

64
Gd
Gadolinium

65
Tb
Terbium

66
Dy
Dysprosium

67
Ho
Holmium

68
Er
Erbium

69
Tm
Thulium

70
Yb
Ytterbium

71
Lu
Lutetium

95
Am
Americium

96
Cm
Curium

97
Bk
Berkelium

98
Cf
Californium

99
Es
Einsteinium

100
Fm
Fermium

101
Md
Mendelevium

102
No
Nobelium

103
Lr
Lawrencium

SCIENTIFIC UNITS

IN AN ATTEMPT TO UNDERSTAND, describe,
and quantify the processes of life, scientists
have created diverse measurements. Units
are standardized to avoid confusion.
Concepts such as energy are measured
using various units because energy is found
in many different forms.

DISTILLATION USING
A CONICAL FLASK

THE pH SCALE
The pH scale measures
acidity or alkalinity with
values of 0–14. Acidic
substances dissolve in
water to form sharp-
tasting solutions that
measure from 0–6.
Alkalis dissolve to give
soapy solutions with a
scale of 8–14.

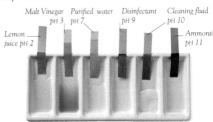

Lemon
juice pH 2

Malt Vinegar
pH 3

Purified water
pH 7

Disinfectant
pH 9

Cleaning fluid
pH 10

Ammonia
pH 11

ELECTRICITY AND MAGNETISM				
QUANTITY	SYMBOL	UNIT	ABBREVIATION	EXPLANATION
Voltage	V	volt	V	A battery/ generator produces a voltage that makes current flow in a circuit.
Current	I	ampere	A	A current is a flow of charged particles, usually electrons.
Resistance	R	ohm	Ω	Resistance is the degree to which a conductor opposes the flow of current.
Energy	E	joule	J	One joule is used every second when 1 amp flows through a resistance of 1 ohm.
Power	P	watt	W	Power is a rate of work done/electricity used. 1 watt is equal to a rate of 1 joule per second.
Charge	Q	coulomb	C	A coulomb is the charge moved in 1 second by a current of 1 amp.

MINERAL HARDNESS

Moh's scale is a measurement of hardness that uses a scale of 1 to 10 to grade minerals.

1 Talc: can be crushed by a fingernail

2 Gypsum: scratched by a fingernail

3 Calcite: scratched by a bronze coin

4 Fluorite: scratched by glass

5 Apatite: scratched by penknife

6 Feldspar: scratched by quartz

7 Quartz: scratched by hard steel file

8 Topaz: scratched by corundum

9 Corundum: scratched by diamond

10 Diamond: scratched only by diamond

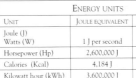

ENERGY UNITS	
UNIT	JOULE EQUIVALENT
Joule (J)	
Watts (W)	1 J per second
Horsepower (Hp)	2,600,000 J
Calories (Kcal)	4,184 J
Kilowatt hour (kWh)	3,600,000 J

British physicist James Joule (1818–89) gave his name to this SI unit. He discovered the first law of thermodynamics (the conservation of energy).

MAGNETIC FIELDS	
FIELD	TESLA (UNIT OF FIELD MEASUREMENT)
Weakest measured field	0.000000000008 T
Earth's field	0.00003 T
Powerful magnet	1 T
Highest field on record	30.1 T

KEY SCIENTISTS

BLAISE PASCAL
Pascal gave his name to units of pressure: one pascal (Pa) is one newton per sq m.

HEINRICH HERTZ
The German physicist demonstrated the existence of radio waves whose unit of frequency (one cycle per second), is named the hertz (Hz).

ANTOINE BECQUEREL
The French physicist is known for his discovery of radioactivity and the units measuring radiation activity, the Becquerel (Bq).

ISAAC NEWTON
The unit of force (that required to accelerate a mass of 1 kg at 1 m /sec) is expressed in newtons (N).

LIGHT AND SOUND

BOTH LIGHT AND SOUND travel as waves through the air. Light forms part of the electromagnetic spectrum, and every different color has a different wavelength. Sound is also identified by different wave frequencies.

LIGHT LAWS

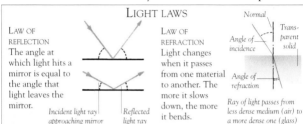

LAW OF REFLECTION
The angle at which light hits a mirror is equal to the angle that light leaves the mirror.

Incident light ray approaching mirror

Reflected light ray

LAW OF REFRACTION
Light changes when it passes from one material to another. The more it slows down, the more it bends.

Normal

Transparent solid

Angle of incidence

Angle of refraction

Ray of light passes from less dense medium (air) to a more dense one (glass)

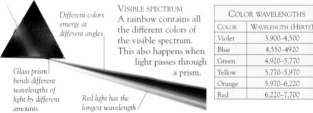

Different colors emerge at different angles

Glass prism bends different wavelengths of light by different amounts

Red light has the longest wavelength

VISIBLE SPECTRUM
A rainbow contains all the different colors of the visible spectrum. This also happens when light passes through a prism.

COLOR WAVELENGTHS	
COLOR	WAVELENGTH (HERTZ)
Violet	3,900–4,500
Blue	4,550–4920
Green	4,920–5,770
Yellow	5,770–5,970
Orange	5,970–6,220
Red	6,220–7,700

ELECTROMAGNETIC SPECTRUM
Different electromagnetic waves have different ranges of wavelength.

Radio waves
100 km–1 mm

Television
0.5 m

Microwaves
0.3 m – 0.001 m

Decibel scale

Sound is created when objects vibrate. The vibrations cause the air to be compressed and contracted into sound waves. The loudness of a sound is measured in decibels.

0 db: Sound you can only just hear

80 db: Pneumatic drill, 66 ft (20 m) away

120 db: Aircraft taking off 330 ft (100 m) away

10 d: Someone whispering 16 ft (5 m) away

100 db: Loud rock concert

130 db: Risk of hearing damage

0 10 20 30 40 50 60 70 80 90 100 110 120 130 140 150

DECIBEL SCALE (db)

SOUND BARRIER

Sometimes aircraft travel faster than the sound they are producing. When this happens, a sonic boom occurs as compressed air at the front of the aircraft breaks to produce a shock wave.

Sonic boom released at speed of sound

SOUND FACTS

- Wavelengths can be as short as one nanometer (nm–one thousand millionth of a meter).

- Bats navigate in flight by emitting high-frequency squeaks.

- Sound travels at about 745 mph1 (1,200 km/h).

SOUND SPEEDS		
Sound travels at different speeds through different materials.		
MATERIAL	SPEED	
	M/SEC	FT/SEC
Rubber	54	177
Air (32°F)	334	1,096
Air (212°F)	366	1,201
Water	1,284	4,213
Mercury	1,452	4,764
Wood	3,580	12,631
Iron/Glass	5,000	16,404

Infra-red 0.0005 m

Ultraviolet rays 1.0 x 10^{-8} m

Visible light 5 x 10^{-7} m

X rays 1.0 x 10^{-11} m

Gamma rays 1 x 1.0^{-13} m

FOOD AND NUTRITION

WHAT WE EAT HAS a huge impact on our health. The study of diet is called nutrition, and it covers all aspects of the relationship of food to the maintenance of bodily functions and health.

VITAL FOOD COMPONENTS

MINERALS	FIBER	CARBOHYDRATES	FATS	PROTEIN
These simple chemicals (e.g., calcium) are not made in the body but are required for its maintenance.	The indigestible part of fruit, vegetables, bread, and cereals, fiber aids normal bowel function.	These are compounds of carbon, oxygen, and hydrogen, such as starch and sugar, that provide energy.	These supply concentrated energy. Also help form chemical "messengers," such as hormones.	This is a substance the body needs for growth and repair. It is found in meat, fish, cheese, and beans.

MAIN VITAMIN SOURCES AND REQUIREMENTS

TYPE OF VITAMIN	WHERE FOUND	REQUIRED FOR
Vitamin A	Liver, fish-liver oils, egg yolk, and yellow-orange colored fruit and vegetables	Growth, healthy eyes and skin, fighting infection.
Vitamin B₁ (Thiamine)	Whole grains (whole-grain bread and pasta) brown rice, liver, beans, peas, and eggs	Healthy functioning of nervous and digestive systems.
Vitamin B₂ (Riboflavin)	Milk, liver, cheese, eggs, green vegetables, brewer's yeast, whole grains, and wheat germ	Metabolism of protein, fat, and carbohydrates. Keeps tissues healthy.
Vitamin B₃ (Niacin)	Liver, lean meats, poultry, fish, nuts, and dried beans	Plentiful energy and healthy, clear skin.
Vitamin B₆ (Pyridoxine)	Liver, poultry, pork, fish, bananas, potatoes, dried beans, and most fruit and vegetables	Metabolism of protein and production of red blood cells.
Vitamin C	Citrus fruit, strawberries, and potatoes	Healthy skin, teeth, bones, and tissues, and for fighting disease.
Vitamin D	Oily fish (e.g., salmon), liver, eggs, cod liver oil, and some cereals	The absorption of calcium and phosphates.
Vitamin E	Margarine, whole grain cereals, and nuts	Formation of new red blood cells. Protection of cell linings in lungs.

FOOD SUPPLY

The "Dietary Energy Supply" (DES) is the amount of food available per person per day, and is measured in calories. This table compares the DES of some countries from around the world.

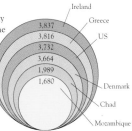

Ireland — 3,837
Greece — 3,816
US — 3,732
Denmark — 3,664
Chad — 1,989
Mozambique — 1,680

METRIC UNITS OF ENERGY

JOULES TO CALORIES INTERNATIONAL		KILOCALORIES INTERNATIONAL TO KILOJOULES		CALORIES INTERNATIONAL TO JOULES		KILOJOULES TO KILOCALORIES INTERNATIONAL	
J	cal	kJ	kcal	cal	J	kcal	kJ
1	0.239	1	0.239	1	4.187	1	4.187
2	0.476	2	0.476	2	8.374	2	8.374
3	0.716	3	0.716	3	12.560	3	12.560
4	0.955	4	0.955	4	16.747	4	16.747
5	1.194	5	1.194	5	20.934	5	20.934
6	1.433	6	1.433	6	25.121	6	25.121
7	1.672	7	1.672	7	29.308	7	29.308
8	1.911	8	1.911	8	33.494	8	33.494
9	2.150	9	2.150	9	37.681	9	37.681
10	2.388	10	2.388	10	41.868	10	41.868
20	4.777	20	4.777	20	83.736	20	83.736
30	7.165	30	7.165	30	125.604	30	125.604
40	9.554	40	9.554	40	167.472	40	167.472
50	11.942	50	11.942	50	209.340	50	209.340
60	14.330	60	14.330	60	251.208	60	251.208
70	16.719	70	16.719	70	293.076	70	293.076
80	19.108	80	19.108	80	334.944	80	334.944
90	21.496	90	21.496	90	367.812	90	367.812
100	23.885	100	23.885	100	418.680	100	418.680

ENERGY CONVERSION

• To convert calories (cal) into joules (J), use the following formula: multiply by 4.187

• To convert joules (J) into calories (cal), use the following formula: multiply by 0.239

• To convert kilocalories (kcal) into kilojoules (kJ), use the following formula: multiply by 4.187

• To convert kilocalories (kJ) into kilocalories (kcal), use the following formula: multiply by x 0.239

MATHEMATICS

NUMBER SYSTEMS

HUMANKIND'S NEED TO COUNT led to the invention of numbers. Systems of counting and their component numbers are the language of mathematics, which has helped to quantify, describe, and explore many aspects of life.

BINARY SYSTEM		
Our number system is based on the number 10, but number systems can be based on any number. The binary system is based on the number 2, and only uses the numbers 0 and 1.	BASE 10 NUMBER	BINARY NUMBER
	1	1
	2	10
	3	11
	4	100
	5	101
	6	110
	7	111
	8	1110

NUMBER SYSTEMS
Early civilizations organized counting systems once trade had advanced beyond barter. Each used different number symbols as dictated by the needs of their society. The Asian Indians and Mayan culture both invented the zero symbol independently.

SYMBOL SYSTEMS					
NUMBER	ROMAN	ARABIC	CHINESE	BABYLONIAN	HINDU
0					
1	I	١	一	𒀹	१
2	II	٢	二	𒀹𒀹	२
3	III	٣	三	𒀹𒀹𒀹	३
4	IV	٤	四	𒀹𒀹𒀹	४
5	V	٥	五	𒀹𒀹𒀹	५
6	VI	٦	六	𒀹𒀹𒀹	६
7	VII	٧	七	𒀹𒀹𒀹	७
8	VIII	٨	八	𒀹𒀹𒀹	८
9	IX	٩	九	𒀹𒀹𒀹	९
10	X	١٠	十	𒌋	१०
50	L	٥٠	五十	≪≪≪	५०
100	C	١٠٠	百	𒁹≪≪≪	१००
500	D	٥٠٠	五百	𒀹𒀹𒀹	५००
1000	M	١٠٠٠	千	𒀹 𒌋	१०००

MATHEMATICAL SYMBOLS

SYMBOL	MEANING	SYMBOL	MEANING
+,	Add (plus)	>	Greater than
−	Subtract (minus)	<	Less than
×	Multiply (times)	≤	Less than or equal to
÷	Divided by	≥	Greater than or equal to
=	Equal to	∞	Infinity
≠	Not equal to	%	Percent

$$3^2 \qquad 4^3 \qquad \sqrt{} \qquad \sqrt[3]{}$$

number squared is ~~equal~~ to n x n	This is shorthand for 4 x 4 x 4	The square root is often written without the 2	The cubed root is the opposite to the cube

~~IN~~DICES, SQUARES, AND ROOTS

~~T~~he index (plural: indices) of a number n is the amount ~~of~~ times the number n is multiplied by itself. A number ~~n~~ squared = n^2 = n x n; n cubed = n^3 = n x n x n; and so ~~o~~n. The opposite of this is the root, i.e., a resultant ~~n~~umber which, when multiplied by the power of the ~~in~~dex, gives the original number n. If $\sqrt[3]{n}$ = m, then m^3 ~~=~~ n; if $\sqrt[2]{n}$ = k, then k^2 = n.

NUMBER FACTS

• Negative numbers were first conceived in China in AD 200.

• The Greeks invented the "Golden ratio," an aesthetic number (1.618), and used it for building proportions in the Parthenon.

• The largest known prime number is 2^{756839} −1, which consists of 227,832 digits.

PRIME NUMBERS

A prime number is only divisible by itself and one, such as 13. Nine is not a prime, since it is divisible by three, as well as by itself and one.

FRACTIONS	STYLE TABLE		
The number above the line in a fraction is called the numerator, and the lower number is the denominator.	FRACTION	DECIMAL	PERCENT
	1/2	0.5	50%
	1/4	0.25	25%
	1/10	0.1	10%
	1/100	0.01	1%

PERCENTAGE	DECIMALS
Percent means "for each hundred" and signifies any fraction with a denominator of 100. So 1/2 is 50/100, or 50%.	Decimals are numbers written in base 10. Numbers after the decimal point are the number of tenths, hundreths, thousandths, etc.

~~S~~LICE AFTER SLICE
~~A~~ cake divided into 8 slices ~~m~~eans each slice equals 1/8.

ARITHMETIC

ROMAN POCKET ABACUS

ARITHMETIC IS THE BASIS of mathematics and initially falls into four categories: addition, subtraction, multiplication, and division. These operation form the core counting system

AN ELECTRONIC CALCULATOR

ADDITION

$$4 + 2 = 6$$

addend | addend | sum

SUBTRACTION

$$24 - 13 = 11$$

minuend | subtrahend | difference

MULTIPLICATION

$$4 \times 3 = 12$$

multiplicand | multiplier | prod

DIVISION

$$44 \div 13 = 3 \text{ r}$$

dividend | divisor | quotient | remaina

CALCULATORS
Calculators range from the abacus to modern electronic models that perform mathematical operations instantly.

HOW TO USE
MULTIPLICATION TABLES
Simply measure off the desired number in the row and match it with the column numbers to give multiplication answers.

MULTIPLICATION TABLE

Row	\	COLUMN										
	1	2	3	4	5	6	7	8	9	10	11	12
1	1	2	3	4	5	6	7	8	9	10	11	12
2	2	4	6	8	10	12	14	16	18	20	22	24
3	3	6	9	12	15	18	21	24	27	30	33	36
4	4	8	12	16	20	24	28	32	36	40	44	48
5	5	10	15	20	25	30	35	40	45	50	55	60
6	6	12	18	24	30	36	42	48	54	60	66	72
7	7	14	21	28	35	42	49	56	63	70	77	84
8	8	16	24	32	40	48	56	64	72	80	88	96
9	9	18	27	36	45	54	63	72	81	90	99	108
10	10	20	30	40	50	60	70	80	90	100	110	120
11	11	22	33	44	55	66	77	88	99	110	121	132
12	12	24	36	48	60	72	84	96	108	120	132	144

Simple and compound interest

Interest refers to money accrued as a credit or debt from a basic amount of borrowed capital. It is calculated as a percentage rate of the original amount. If a person places money in a bank, then the bank pays the customer interest on the money; if a person borrows money from a bank, then the person pays the bank interest.

SIMPLE INTEREST
This type of interest is calculated in respect to the original amount of money borrowed, or invested, which is called the principal.

COMPOUND INTEREST
While simple interest is paid only on the principal, compound interest is paid on the principal and the interest as it is earned and added onto the principal.

$$\text{Total sum} = P\left(1 + \frac{i \times n}{100}\right)$$

P is the principal,
i is the percentage of interest,
n is number of time periods.

$$S = P \times (1+i)^n$$

P is the principal,
i is the periodic interest rate,
and n is the number of time periods.

EXAMPLE
If $100 is borrowed or lent for 1 year at 7 percent (%) per annum (year), the total sum would be calculated as follows:
P = 100, R= 7, T = 1.
Total Sum = $100+ \left(\dfrac{100 \times 7 \times 1}{100}\right)$

$$= 100 + 7$$
$$= \$107$$

EXAMPLE
If $100 is borrowed or lent for 2 years at 7 percent (%) per annum (year), the total sum would be calculated as follows:
$$= 100 \times (1 + 0.07)^2$$
$$= 100 \times (1.07)^2$$
$$= 100 \times 1.1449$$
$$= \$114.49$$

GEOMETRY

THE MATHEMATICAL STUDY of figures and solid shapes uses lines, angles, and surfaces to examine properties.

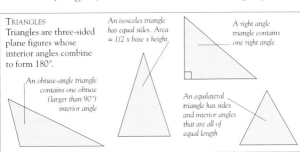

TRIANGLES
Triangles are three-sided plane figures whose interior angles combine to form 180°.

An isosceles triangle has equal sides. Area = 1/2 x base x height

A right angle triangle contains one right angle

An obtuse-angle triangle contains one obtuse (larger than 90°) interior angle

An equilateral triangle has sides and interior angles that are all of equal length

POLYGONS
These are shapes that have many (three or more) angles and sides.

Square: all sides and angles are the same length

Hexagon: polygon with six sides

Pentagon polygon with five sides

Octagon: polygon with eight sides

Quadrilateral: four-sided polygon

POLYGONS		
NAME	NO OF SIDES	INTERNAL ANGLES
Triangle	3	60°
Quadrilateral	4	90°
Pentagon	5	108°
Hexagon	6	120°
Heptagon	7	128.6°
Octagon	8	135°
Nonagon	9	140°
Decagon	10	144°
Undecagon	11	147.3°
Dodecagon	12	150°

PLANE FIGURES

These are two-dimensional (flat) shapes, such as a quadrilaterals or polygons, that are plane figures with three or more straight sides.

Rectangle: quadrilateral with opposite sides of equal length that meet at right angles. Area = base x height

Rhombus: quadrilateral with sides of equal length. Area = 1/2 x (a x b)

Trapezium: quadrilateral with only two sides parallel. Area =1/2 x sum of parallel sides x distance between them

Parallelogram: quadrilateral with opposite sides of equal length. Area = a x b

---

SOLIDS

Solids are three-dimensional shapes. Polyhedrons are solids that have plane (flat) faces.

Cone: Circular base, narrowing to a point, or apex. Volume = 1/3 x π x radius² x height

Apex

Cylinder: two circular faces, connected by a tube. Surface area = π x diameter x length. Volume π x radius² x length

Rectangular block: volume = length x breadth x height

Tetrahedron: polyhedron with four triangles as faces

Sphere: globe-shaped figure with every point equidistant from the center

Cubes: polyhedrons with 6 sides of equal length, shape, and area

Octahedron: tetrahedron with eight flat sides

Hemisphere: half of a sphere

Triangular prism: solid figure with two triangular ends. Volume = area of ends x distance between them

Square pyramid: tetrahedron with square base and four triangular sides

Spheroid: egg-shaped figure

ANGLES AND CIRCLES

AN ANGLE IS THE MEASURE of space between two lines on a flat surface (or three planes in a solid) that join at a common point. Angles are measured in degrees (°), or radians. When one angle has passed through 360°, it has formed a complete circle.

ANATOMY OF A CIRCLE
A circle is a closed curve on which all points are equidistant from the center. Its diameter passes from one side to another through this center point. Its ratio to the circumference is a expressed by Pi (π) or 3.141592.

Chord: a straight line joining any two points on the circumference

Segment: part of a circle between a chord and the circumference

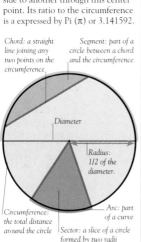

Diameter

Radius: 1/2 of the diameter.

Circumference: the total distance around the circle

Arc: part of a curve

Sector: a slice of a circle formed by two radii

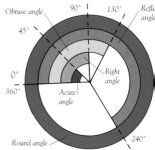

Obtuse angle
90° 130° Reflex angle
45°
Right angle
0°
360°
Acute angle
Round angle
240°

DEGREES OF A CIRCLE
The hands of a clock form an angle between each other. As they move apart, that angle increases.

TYPES OF ANGLE	
TYPE	MEASUREMENT
Acute angle	angle between 0° – 90°
Right angle	angle measures exactly 90°
Obtuse angle	angle between 90° – 180°
Reflex angle	angle between 180° – 360°
Complementary angles	2 angles that add up to 90°
Supplementary angles	2 angles that add up to 180°
Conjugate angles	2 angles that add up to 360°

Trigonometry

Trigonometry is used to solve problems concerning right-angled triangles. Since there is a fixed angle, ratios exist that affect the relationships of the other angles and the lengths of their sides.

TRIGONOMETRY CALCULATION

To find the height of the tower, multiply the tangent (tan) of the angle from the point of the observer to the top of the tower (40°) by the distance from the tower (2,162 ft). This gives a height of 583 m.

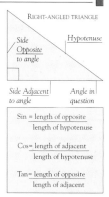

RIGHT-ANGLED TRIANGLE

Side Opposite to angle

Hypotenuse

Side Adjacent to angle

Angle in question

$$Sin = \frac{length\ of\ opposite}{length\ of\ hypotenuse}$$

$$Cos = \frac{length\ of\ adjacent}{length\ of\ hypotenuse}$$

$$Tan = \frac{length\ of\ opposite}{length\ of\ adjacent}$$

TRIGONOMIC RATIOS

Since the hypotenuse always remains opposite the right angle, then this forms the basis for the ratios of angles and sides.

Position of observer

2,162 ft (695 m)   40°

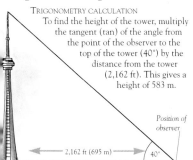

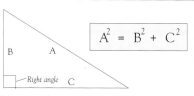

$$A^2 = B^2 + C^2$$

B   *A*

Right angle   *C*

PYTHAGORAS'S THEOREM

This states that for any right-angled triangle, the squares of the two sides adjacent to the right angle (B and C) are equal to the square of the hypotenuse (A, the longest side of the triangle).

MATHEMATICS FACTS

• The theorem that bears the name of the Greek mathematician Pythagoras was known by the Babylonians and Egyptians hundreds of years earlier.

• The terms "*algorithm*" and "*algebra*" come from al-Khwarizmi, the Arab mathematician.

WEIGHTS AND MEASURES

TWO MAJOR SYSTEMS OF MEASUREMENT exist: metric and imperial. Although some countries still use the older imperial system, scientists worldwide use metric

THE SEVEN BASE SI UNITS			
SI (Système Internationale d'Unités) is the standard system of units for scientists worldwide. There are seven base units, from which the other units are derived.	QUANTITY	SYMBOL	UNIT
	Mass	kg	Kilogram
	Length	m	Meter
	Time	s	Second
	Electric current	A	Ampere
	Temperature	K	Kelvin
	Luminous intensity	cd	Candela
	Amount of substance	mol	Mole

IMPERIAL & USCS UNIT
Imperial units include the pound, mile, and gallon. With no scientific basis, it is a complex system. In the US, this system is called USCS (US Customary Systems).

STANDARD KILOGRAM

STANDARDS
Several units have precisely defined standards. This ensures that everyone means the same thing when stating measurements.

THE STANDARD SECOND
One second is defined as "the duration of 9,192,631,770 periods of the radiation corresponding to the transition between the hyperfine levels of the ground state of the cesium-133 atom."

THE STANDARD KILOGRAM
A standard kilogram is kept in carefully controlled conditions a the Bureau of Weights and measures at Sèvres, France.

THE STANDARD METER
One meter is defined as "the length equal to the 1,650,763.7 wavelengths, in a vacuum, of th radiation corresponding to the transition between the levels 2p and 5d5 of the krypton-86 atom

NUMBER TERMS GREAT AND SMALL*					
PREFIX	SYMBOL	MEANING	PREFIX	SYMBOL	MEANING
tera	T	One trillion	deci	d	One-tenth
giga	G	One billion	denti	c	One-hundredth
mega	M	One million	milli	m	One-thousandth
kilo	k	One thousand	micro	µ	One-millionth
hecto	h	One hundred	nano	n	One-billionth

*Prefixes inserted before a unit signify multiples or fractions of that unit.

Adjustable jaw

MEASURING
SOLIDS

Calipers are used
to find the width of
solid objects.

LENGTH	
METRIC	
1 millimeter (mm)	
1 centimeter (cm)	10 mm
1 meter (m)	100 cm
1 kilometer (km)	1,000 m
IMPERIAL	
1 inch (in)	
1 foot (ft)	12 in
1 yard (yd)	3 ft
1 mile	1,760 yd

MEASUREMENT FACTS

• France was the first
country to adopt the
metric system. King
Louis XVI approved it
in 1791, the day before
he tried to flee
the Revolution.

• China was the first
country to use a
decimal system.
Wooden rulers divided
into units of ten have
been found and dated
to the 6th century.

• In England, the
length of a human top
thumb-joint was a
widely used measure
that became the
precursor of the inch.

MASS AND WEIGHT	
METRIC	
1 gram (g)	
1 kilogram (kg)	1,000 g
1 tonne (t)	1,000 kg
IMPERIAL	
1 ounce (oz)	
1 pound (lb)	16 oz
1 stone	14 lb
1 hundredweight (cwt)	8 stones
1 ton	20 cwt

LIQUID MEASURES
Measuring jugs are used to
find the volumes of liquids.

AREA	
METRIC	
1 square millimeter (sq mm)	
1 square centimeter (sq cm)	100 sq mm
1 square meter (sq m)	10,000 sq cm
1 hectare (ha)	10,000 sq m
1 square kilometer (sq km)	1,000,000 sq m
IMPERIAL	
1 square inch (sq in)	
1 square foot (sq ft)	144 sq in
1 square yard (sq yd)	9 sq ft
1 acre	4,840 sq yd
1 square mile	640 acres

VOLUME	
METRIC	
1 cubic millimeter (cu mm)	
1 cubic centimeter (cu cm)	1,000 cu mm
1 cubic meter (cu m)	1,000,000 cu cm
1 liter	1,000 cu cm
IMPERIAL	
1 cubic inch (cu in)	
1 cubic foot (cu ft)	1,728 cu in
1 cubic yard (cu yd)	27 cu ft
1 fluid ounce (fl oz)	
1 pint (pt)	20 fl oz
1 gallon (gal)	8 pt

CONVERSION TABLES

FOOT RULE

LENGTH CONVERSION		
TO CONVERT:	INTO:	MULTIPLY BY:
IMPERIAL	METRIC	
Inches	Centimeters	2.54
Feet	Meters	0.3048
Yards	Meters	0.9144
Miles	Kilometers	1.6093
METRIC	IMPERIAL	
Centimeters	Inches	0.3937
Meters	Feet	3.2808
Meters	Yards	1.0936
Kilometers	Miles	0.6214
Meters	Furlongs	0.005
Meters	Fathoms	0.547
Kilometers	Nautical miles	0.54
Meters	Chains	0.0497

VOLUME CONVERSION		
TO CONVERT:	INTO:	MULTIPLY BY:
IMPERIAL	METRIC	
Cubic inches	Cubic cm (ml)	16.3871
Cubic feet	Litres	28.3169
Cubic yards	Cubic meters	0.7646
Fluid ounces	Cubic cm (ml)	28.413
Pints	Liters	0.5683
Gallons	Liters	4.5461
METRIC	IMPERIAL	
Cubic cm	Cubic inches	0.061
(milliliters)	Fluid ounces	0.0352
Liters	Cubic feet	0.0353
Cubic meters	Cubic yards	1.308
Liters	Pints	1.7598
	Gallons	0.22

AREA CONVERSION		
TO CONVERT:	INTO:	MULTIPLY BY:
IMPERIAL	METRIC	
Sq inches	Sq centimeters	6.4516
Sq feet	Sq meters	0.0929
Sq yards	Sq meters	0.8361
Acres	Hectares	0.4047
Sq miles	Sq kilometers	2.59
METRIC	IMPERIAL	
Sq centimeters	Sq inches	0.155
Sq meters	Sq feet	10.7639
Sq meters	Sq yards	1.196
Hectares	Acres	2.4711
Sq kilometers	Sq miles	0.3861

MASS AND WEIGHT CONVERSIONS		
TO CONVERT:	INTO:	MULTIPLY BY:
IMPERIAL	METRIC	
Ounces	Grams	28.3495
Pounds	Kilograms	0.4536
Stones	Kilograms	6.3503
Hundredweights	Kilograms	50.802
Tons	Tonnes	0.9072
METRIC	IMPERIAL	
Grams	Ounces	0.0352
Kilograms	Pounds	2.2046
	Stones	0.1575
	Hundredweights	0.0197
Tonnes	Tons	1.1023

COOKING MEASURES

Object	Metric	Imperial
1 thimble	2.5 ml	30 drops
60 drops	5 ml	1 teaspoon
1 teaspoon	5 ml	1 dram
1 desert spoon	10 ml	2 drams
1 tablespoon	20 ml	4 drams
2 tablespoons	40 ml	1 fl oz
1 wine glass	100 ml	2 fl oz
1 tea cup	200 ml	5 fl oz (1 gill)
1 mug	400 ml	10 fl oz

2.5 ML (1/2 TEASPOON)

OVEN TEMPERATURES

Gas mark*	Electricity		Rating
(* not US)	°C	°F	
1/2	120	250	Slow
1	140	275	-
2	150	300	-
3	170	325	-
4	180	350	Moderate
5	190	375	-
6	200	400	Hot
7	220	425	-
8	230	450	Very hot
9	260	500	-

FAHRENHEIT TO CELSIUS TO KELVIN

°F	°C	K	°F	°C	K	°F	°C	K
–4.0	–20	253	32.0	0	273	68.0	20	293
–2.2	–19	254	33.8	1	274	69.8	21	294
–0.4	–18	255	35.6	2	275	71.6	22	295
1.4	–17	256	37.4	3	276	73.4	23	296
3.2	–16	257	39.2	4	277	75.2	24	297
5.0	–15	258	41.0	5	278	77.0	25	298
6.8	–14	259	42.8	6	279	78.8	26	299
8.6	–13	260	44.6	7	280	80.6	27	300
10.4	–12	261	46.4	8	281	82.4	28	301
12.2	–11	262	48.2	9	282	84.2	29	302
14.0	–10	263	50.0	10	283	86.0	30	303
15.8	–9	264	51.8	11	284	87.8	31	304
17.6	–8	265	53.6	12	285	89.6	32	305
19.4	–7	266	55.4	13	286	91.4	33	306
21.2	–6	267	57.2	14	287	93.2	34	307
23.0	–5	268	59.0	15	288	95.0	35	308
24.8	–4	269	60.8	16	289	96.8	36	309
26.6	–3	270	62.6	17	290	98.6	37	310
28.4	–2	271	64.4	18	291	100.4	38	311
30.2	–1	272	66.2	19	292	102.2	39	312

TEMPERATURES

- To convert Fahrenheit (°F) into Celsius (°C), use the following formula:
$$°C = (°F - 32) ÷ 1.8$$
- To convert Celsius (°C) into Fahrenheit (°F), use the following formula:
$$°F = (°C \times 1.8) + 32$$
- To convert Celsius (°C) into Kelvin (K), use the following formula:
$$K = °C + 273.16$$

Thermometers measure temperature on Celsius and Fahrenheit scales

SPEED

AN INCREASE IN speed allows an object to travel faster and cover distances more quickly. For many animals, this may mean the difference between life and death. For humankind, being able to travel quickly is a luxury that allows us to make more of our lives.

RACING YACHT

KNOT CONVERSION

To convert:	Into:	Multiply by:
Metric:		
Knots	km/h	1.852
Km/h	knots	0.540
Imperial:		
Knots	mph	1.151
Mph	knots	1.001
Knots	feet/sec	1.688

TABLE OF MECHANICAL SPEED RECORDS

RECORD DESCRIPTION	VEHICLE NAME	SPEED MPH
Land	*Thrust II*	633
Water	*Spirit of Australia*	319
Air (by air launch)	X-15A	4,534
Land (unmanned)	US Air Force rocket sled	3,061
Air (by take off)	Lockheed SR17a Blackbird	2,193

X-15A

SPEED FACT BOX

• Peregrine falcons can reach 217 mph (350 km/h) in a dive.

• Airliner Concorde cruises at 1,354 mph (2,179 km/h).

SPEED CONVERSIONS

To convert:	Into:	Multiply by:
Kilometers per hour	miles per hour	0.621
Miles per hour	Kilometers per hour	1.609
	Meters per second	0.447
Meters per second	Miles per hour	2.237
Feet per second	Miles per hour	0.681

ANIMAL SPEEDS

Animals are capable of great speeds, which they use to chase prey or escape predators. By comparison, even the fastest human sprinters lag far behind.

FASTEST BIRD

Spine-tailed swift can reach a speed of 106 mph (171 km/h)

FASTEST ON LAND

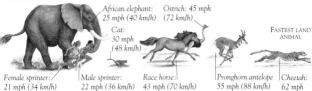

African elephant: 25 mph (40 km/h)

Cat: 30 mph (48 km/h)

Ostrich: 45 mph (72 km/h)

FASTEST LAND ANIMAL

Female sprinter: 21 mph (34 km/h)

Male sprinter: 22 mph (36 km/h)

Race horse: 43 mph (70 km/h)

Pronghorn antelope 55 mph (88 km/h)

Cheetah: 62 mph (100 km/h)

FASTEST IN WATER

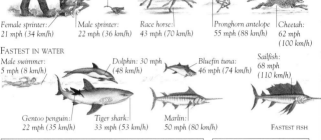

Male swimmer: 5 mph (8 km/h)

Dolphin: 30 mph (48 km/h)

Bluefin tuna: 46 mph (74 km/h)

Sailfish: 68 mph (110 km/h)

Gentoo penguin: 22 mph (35 km/h)

Tiger shark: 33 mph (53 km/h)

Marlin: 50 mph (80 km/h)

FASTEST FISH

WIND SPEED: THE BEAUFORT SCALE		
FORCE	SPEED	DAMAGE
Force 1	2 mph (3 km/h)	smoke drifts
Force 2	5 mph (9 km/h)	leaves rustle
Force 3	10 mph (15 km/h)	flags flutter
Force 4	15 mph (25 km/h)	small branches move
Force 5	21 mph (35 km/h)	small trees sway
Force 6	28 mph (45 km/h)	large branches move
Force 7	35 mph (56 km/h)	whole trees sway
Force 8	43 mph (68 km/h)	twigs break
Force 9	50 mph (81 km/h)	branches break
Force 10	59 mph (94 km/h)	trees blow down
Force 11	69 mph (110 km/h)	serious damage
Force 12	74 mph (118 km/h)	hurricane damage

WIND FACT BOX

• The world wind speed record of 231 mph (371 km/h) was recorded in 1934 on Mt. Washington.

• Tornadoes are known to reach speeds of up to 280 mph (450 km/h).

• Over 1 month, Port Martin, Antarctica, had a mean wind speed of 65 mph (105 km/h).

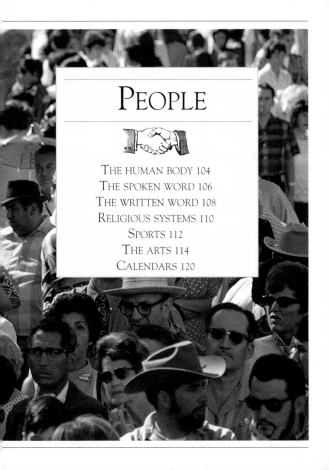

PEOPLE

THE HUMAN BODY

EACH PERSON CONSISTS of a set of body systems. Each system uses organs that cooperate to make the body function. Cells, the basic units of life, divide and multiply to produce the different types of tissues used to make the body's organs. The body contains about 50 billion cells, which are continually being replaced.

THE SKELETON

The skeleton consists of 206 bones (babies have over 300), which support the body and provide points of attachment for the muscles. They are lighter and five times stronger than a steel bar of the same weight. Bones also manufacture red blood cells and store calcium.

The average human brain weighs 1.4 kg, and contains about 15 billion nerve cells. About 0.85 liters of blood pass through the brain every minute

Colour vision is so sensitive that some people can distinguish 300,000 different shades

The lungs contain over 300 million air sacs (alveoli) and have an average 5 litre air capacity

A person's heart beats about 37 million times a year, pumping the weight of 3,300 tons of blood a day

The stomach contains hydrochloric acid to break down food and kill germs

The small intestine, used to absorb food, is around 9 ft (2.8m) long

There are 27 bones in each hand

The femur (thighbone) is the longest and strongest bone in the body. The smallest is the stirrup (stapes) bone in the ear

The total length of blood vessels in the average adult is 100,000 miles

AVERAGE PEOPLE
The average vital statistics are as follows:
Height: man – 5 ft 6 in
woman – 5 ft 3 in
Weight: man – 162 lb
woman – 135 lb
Waist: man – 32 in
woman – 29 in
Hips: man – 39 in
woman – 39 in

THE MUSCULAR SYSTEM
Muscles carry out the body's movements. They work in opposing pairs and can contract to one-third their size. There are 639 muscles in the body, which account for 40 percent of its weight.

THE SKIN
Skin is the body's protective coating. It is waterproof, bacteria-proof, and self-repairing. Nerve cells detect stimuli; over 3 million pores regulate body temperature. Skin also produces hair and nails from keratin, its protective protein.

THE CIRCULATORY SYSTEM
The circulation pumps blood around the body by means of the heart. A continuous circuit feeds oxygen to and from red blood cells via a network of arteries and veins. This network sends blood to the vital organs and carries chemical-rich plasma throughout the body.

THE NERVOUS SYSTEM
The nervous system is the communications network of the body. Stimuli send nerve impulses traveling at over 200 mph (320 km/h) across the body. Impulse messages are sent via the spinal cord to be translated and responded to by the brain.

THE SPOKEN WORD

PEOPLE USE LANGUAGES, organized systems of sound
that express thought, to communicate with each
other. It is believed that the many global dialects stem
from a few root languages: people in India and Iran
share the same linguistic heritage as Europeans.

KEY

Arabic

Chinese

English

French

Portuguese

Russian

Spanish

Hindi

Others

*The Inuit of the
Arctic circle speak
"Inuktituit," a
language belonging
to the Eskimo-
Aleut group that
has around
60,000 speakers*

*Spanish is estimate
to be the world
fastest-growin
language, becaus
of Latin America
burgeonin
population growt*

*Amerindian languages such
as Chinook and Nookta are
polysynthetic in that they
use long and complex
words to express the
meanings of whole phrases*

MOST COMMON LANGUAGES		
LANGUAGE	NO. OF SPEAKERS	HOW TO SAY YES AND NO
Chinese (Mandarin)	1,093 million	Shi	Bu shi
English	450 million	Yes	No
Hindi	367 million	Haan	Nahi
Spanish	352 million	Si	No
Russian	204 million	Dah	Nyet
Arabic	202 million	Na'am	La'a
Bengali	187 million	Haa	Naa
Portuguese	175 million	Sim	Não
Malay-Indonesian	145 million	Ya	Tidak
Japanese	126 million	Hai	Lie

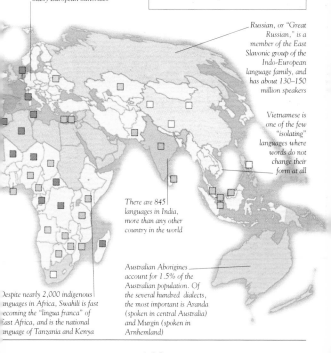

Germany has 75 million first-language speakers, the largest number in the European Union. It is spoken in Germany, Switzerland, and Austria, and by many European minorities

LANGUAGES OF THE WORLD
Between 5,000–10,000 languages and dialects exist in the world. This number is shrinking as indigenous dialects disappear in favor of unifying national languages. Some languages, like English, have become truly international.

Russian, or "Great Russian," is a member of the East Slavonic group of the Indo-European language family, and has about 130–150 million speakers

Vietnamese is one of the few "isolating" languages where words do not change their form at all

There are 845 languages in India, more than any other country in the world

Australian Aborigines account for 1.5% of the Australian population. Of the several hundred dialects, the most important is Aranda (spoken in central Australia) and Murgin (spoken in Arnhemland)

Despite nearly 2,000 indigenous languages in Africa, Swahili is fast becoming the "lingua franca" of East Africa, and is the national language of Tanzania and Kenya

THE WRITTEN WORD

WRITING BEGAN as pictures that related to objects or ideas. Later, writing systems arose that mirrored the spoken languages: logographic (signs for each word), syllabic (signs for syllables), and alphabetic (signs for each sound).

EAGLE		OWL	
REED		SNAIL	
ARM		SHUTTER	
DOUBLE REED		WATER	

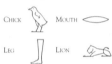

CHICK		MOUTH	
LEG		LION	

HIEROGLYPHS
The ancient Egyptians used complex pictographic writing to adorn tombs and temples. The word hieroglyphics means "sacred carvings."

CUNEIFORM
The Sumerians of Mesopotamia invented the oldest known script, cuneiform, around 3100 BC. The name refers to the wedge-shaped strokes used to form characters.

MEANING	3000 BC	2400 BC	650 BC
BIRD			
HAND			
HEAD			
REED			
WALK OR STAND			
WATER			

CHINESE
The Chinese language uses a logographic system that derived from unique pictograms. Symbols became stylized into meaning a sounding word rather than just the image. For this, many characters are needed to express every word in the language. Chinese has 2–3,000 common characters, although the total number in use is about 50,000.

日 + 月 = 明
SUN MOON BRIGHT

一 ONE
小 LITTLE
日 SUN

上 GO UP
天 SKY
月 MOON

心 HEART 去 TO GO
汁 JUICE 冰 ICE
魚 FISH 信 LETTER

BURDEN

VULTURE

MAYAN

Of the 13 Mesoamerican writing systems identified, Mayan is the fullest. Symbols stood for objects or concepts, reflecting the Mayan preoccupation with time and the universe.

WEST

SOUTH

FACT BOX

• "O," the oldest letter, has not changed its form since it was part of the early Phoenician alphabet in 1600 BC.

CYRILLIC

А Б В Г Д Е Ж З И Й К Л
М Н О П Р С Т У Ф Х Ц Ч
Ш Щ Ъ Ы Ь Ѣ Э Ю Я Ѵ

The Cyrillic alphabet is named after St. Cyril who spread the Christian faith to the Slavonic peoples in AD 800.

HINDI

Of the 200 scripts derived from the Devanagari script, Hindi is used as the national written word.

अ आ इ ई उ ऊ

ऋ ए ऐ ओ औ क ख ग घ ङ च छ ज

झ ञ ट ठ ड ढ ण त थ द ध न प फ ब

भ म य र ल व श ष स ह

Individual alphabet letters translate every sound

PHOENICIAN	✕	𐤒	𐤀	𐤄	𐤉		𐤆	𐤇	⊗	Z		⅄	L	₼	𐤉	∄	‡	O	𐤒	𐤒	٩	𐤔	✗	𐤕
HEBREW	א	ב	ג	ד	ה		ז	ח	ט	י		כ	ל	מ	נ	ס	ע	פ	צ	ק	ר	ש	ת	
EARLY GREEK	∀	8	1	⅃	∃	Ⅎ		⊟	⊗	I		⅄	𐤉	₼	५	∄		O	⊓	Ϻ	٩	٢	⟨	✗
CLASSICAL GREEK	A	B	Γ	Δ	E		Z	H	Θ	I		K	Λ	M	N	Ξ	O	Π		Ρ	Σ	T	Υ	Φ ✗ Ψ Ω
ETRUSCAN	A	8	⅂	𐌃	∃	Ⅎ		⊟	⊗	I		⅄	𐌋	₼	И	⊞	O	⅂	Ϻ	𐌐	٩	٢		✗
ROMAN	A	B	C	D	E	F	G		H	I		K	L	M	N		O	P		Q	R	S	T	V		X		Y Z

DEVELOPMENT OF ALPHABETS

Basing their script on the Phoenician syllabary, the ancient Greeks invented the alphabet by introducing vowel signs that were separate from consonants. This became the source of modern alphabets.

RELIGIOUS SYSTEMS

RELIGIONS EVOLVED through people's desire to understand their place in the universe and give meaning to their lives. Cultures express their beliefs in many different ways, reinforcing faith with the ritual of worship.

TOP SIX FAITHS	
FAITH	NUMBER OF FOLLOWERS
Christianity	1,833 million
Islam	971 million
Hinduism	733 million
Buddhism	315 million
Sikhism	13.5–16 million
Judaism	13–14.3 million

CHRISTIANITY

Christians believe in a historical figure called Jesus. They believe that, as the son of God, he brought teachings that were validated by his resurrection from the dead.

COMMUNION CUP

CHRISTIAN HOLY DAYS	
NAME	EVENT
Christmas	The birthday of Jesus Christ
Good Friday	Jesus is crucified on a cross
Easter	Jesus is resurrected from the dead
Pentecost	Descent of the Holy Spirit
Palm Sunday	Entry of Jesus into Jerusalem

ISLAM

Islam preaches that there is only one god, Allah. His followers, Muslims, study codes set out in the *Koran*, a divine text distilled by the prophet Muhammad.

BOOK OF ISLAM

ISLAMIC FESTIVALS	
NAME	EVENT
Mawlid al-Nabi	Birthday of Muhammad
Layl'at al-Quadr	Koran revealed to Muhammad
Id al-Fitr	Celebration of end of Ramadan
Id al-Adha	Celebration in memory of Abraham's sacrifice

HINDUISM

Hindus worship many gods, which reflects belief in life's diversity. Believers who live good lives are born again into a higher life.

BRAHMA

HINDU HOLY DAYS	
NAME	EVENT
Diwali	New Year Festival of Lights
Holi	Spring Festival
Janmashtami	Birthday of Krishna
Shiva Ratri	Main festival of Shiva

BUDDHISM

Siddhartha Gautama, the Buddha, was an historical figure who taught that desires are the cause of suffering. Many different forms of Buddhism exist in Asia.

THE BUDDHA

BUDDHIST HOLY DAYS	
NAME	EVENT
Wesak	Birthday of the Buddha
Dhammacakka	The Buddha's first sermon
Bodhi Day	Buddha's enlightenment
Parinirvana	The Buddha's liberation
Phagguna	Origin of life cycle

SIKHISM

Sikhism originated in the Punjab area of the Indian subcontinent in 1500. It is based on a unity of God as taught by the ten Sikh gurus who established Sikhism.

GOLDEN TEMPLE OF AMRITSAR

SIKH HOLY DAYS	
NAME	EVENT
Baisakhi	New year and formation of Khalsa
Diwali	Release from prison of Guru Hargobind, the sixth Guru
Guru Nanak	Birthday of the founder
Hola Mohalla	Three day festival held during Holi

JUDAISM

The oldest living religion is based on the one god as revealed in the Hebrew Bible. Its followers, the Jews, have a mission to transmit God's message.

THE HAND OF GOD

JEWISH HOLY DAYS	
NAME	EVENT
Hannukah	Festival of Lights
Pesach/Passover	Rescue from slavery in Egypt
Yom Kippur	Day of Atonement
Rosh Hashana	New Year

OTHER RELIGIONS		
NAME	FOUNDED	FAITH
Baha'i Faith	Persia, 19th c. BC	Worships one god who is at the root of all religions
Confucianism	China, 6th c. BC	Not based on worship of a god but on an approach to life that seeks to conform to the "Will of Heaven," life's ruling principle
Jainism	India, 6th c. BC	Established with the principle of "ahimsa," or nonviolence, Jains believe in a soul but not in a god
Shintoism	Japan, 8th c. BC	Based on the worship of the gods and spirits of nature
Taoism	China, 4th c. BC	Balances life with the "Tao," the mystical power behind events
Zoroastrianism	Persia, 1000 BC	Based on a constant struggle between a good god (Ahura Mazda) and an evil god (Ahriman)

SPORTS

ALTHOUGH THE ORIGINS of competitive sports are obscure, the Greeks first held their Olympic Games in 776 BC. In 1896, the Olympics were revived, with most developments occurring since then. Today, organized sports take place on both national and global levels.

OLYMPIC SYMBOL
The five interlocking rings symbolize Asia, Africa, Europe, America, and Australia.

SUMMER OLYMPIC GAMES venues					
YEAR	VENUE	YEAR	VENUE	YEAR	VENUE
1896	Athens, Greece	1932	Los Angeles, US	1972	Munich, Germany
1900	Paris, France	1936	Berlin, Germany	1976	Montreal, Canada
1904	St. Louis, US	1948	London, England	1980	Moscow, USSR
1908	London, England	1952	Helsinki, Finland	1984	Los Angeles, US
1912	Stockholm, Sweden	1956	Melbourne, Australia	1988	Seoul, South Korea
1920	Antwerp, Belgium	1960	Rome, Italy	1992	Barcelona, Spain
1924	Paris, France	1964	Tokyo, Japan	1996	Atlanta, US
1928	Amsterdam, Holland	1968	Mexico City, Mexico	2000	Sydney, Australia

WINTER OLYMPIC GAMES venues					
YEAR	VENUE	YEAR	VENUE	YEAR	VENUE
1924	Chamonix, France	1960	Squaw Valley, US	1988	Calgary, Canada
1928	St. Moritz, Switzerland	1964	Innsbruch, Austria	1992	Albertville, France
1932	Lake Placid, US	1968	Grenoble, France	1994	Lillehammer, Norway
1936	Garmisch, Germany	1972	Sapporo, Japan	1998	Nagano, Japan
1948	St. Moritz, Switzerland	1976	Innsbruck, Austria	2002	Salt Lake City, US
1952	Oslo, Norway	1980	Lake Placid, US	During the two world wars the	
1956	Cortina, Italy	1984	Sarajevo, Yugoslavia	Games were not held.	

WORLD SERIES: BASEBALL

Baseball is the national sport of the United States. Each year, the top two teams play each other in a competition known as the World Series. The contest is won on a 'best of seven games' basis.

TEAM	WINS
New York Yankees	22
St. Louis Cardinal's	9
Philadelphia/ Kansas City/ Oakland Athletics	9
Brooklyn/ Los Angeles Dodgers	6
Boston Red Sox	5
Pittsburgh Pirates	5
New York/ San Francisco Giants	5
Cincinnati Reds	5

FOOTBALL WORLD CUP

YEAR	VENUE	WINNER
1930	Uruguay	Uruguay
1934	Italy	Italy
1938	France	Italy
1950	Brazil	Uruguay
1954	Switzerland	W. Germany
1958	Sweden	Brazil
1962	Chile	Brazil
1966	England	England
1970	Mexico	Brazil
1974	W. Germany	W. Germany
1978	Argentina	Argentina
1982	Spain	Italy
1986	Mexico	Argentina
1990	Italy	W. Germany
1994	US	Brazil

TENNIS TOURNAMENTS

TOURNAMENT	PLACE	SURFACE
Wimbledon	London, England	Grass
United Stated Open	Flushing Meadow, New York, US	Artificial material
Australian Open	Nat. Tennis Center, Melbourne, Australia	Synthetic
French Open	Roland Garros Stadium, Paris, France	Grass

To win the grand slam is to hold all these titles simultaneously.

MAJOR GOLF TOURNAMENTS

TOURNAMENT	FIRST HELD	TOURNAMENT	FIRST HELD
British Open	1860	Ryder Cup	1927
US Open	1895	Curtis Cup	1932
US PGA	1916	US Masters	1934

Ryder and Curtis Cup are male and female team events.

SORTS FACTS

• In 1954, Britain's Roger Bannister was the first man to run a sub-4 minute mile.

• The first man to run 100m in under 10 seconds was Jim Hines of the US in 1968.

• In 1935, Jesse Owens of the US set six Olympic records in only 45 minutes.

• The puck in ice hockey can reach speeds of up to 118 mph (190 km/h).

THE ARTS

EVERY CULTURE EXPRESSES itself through art. From the earliest cave paintings of prehistoric times to pop-art sculptures, humankind has invented many art forms. In western culture, art has moved beyond its expressive role in society to become a valued –and valuable– commodity. This has led to a cult of fine art, which is closely monitored by art historians.

PORTRAIT OF DR. GACHET
This masterpiece was painted by Van Gogh in 1890 at the village of Auvers-sur-Oise, near Paris.

POPULAR EUROPEAN GALLERIES	
ART GALLERY	VISITORS
Louvre, Paris	5,000,000
Prado, Madrid	1,828,058
Uffizi Gallery, Florence	1,020,972
Van Gogh Museum, Amsterdam	850,952
National Gallery, London	575,880
Alte Pinakothek, Munich	325,084

MOST EXPENSIVE PAINTINGS SOLD AT AUCTION	
TITLE, ARTIST, DATE SOLD	PRICE IN US$
Portrait of Dr. Gachet, Van Gogh, 1990	82,500,000
Au moulin de la galette, Renoir, 1990	78,100,000
Irises, Van Gogh, 1987	53,900,000
Les noces de pierrette, Picasso, 1989	51,895,000
Self portrait: Yo Picasso, Picasso, 1989	47,850,000
Au lapin agile, Picasso, 1989	40,700,000
Sunflowers, Van Gogh, 1987	40,342,500
Portrait of Cosimo I de Medici, Pontormo, 1989	35,200,000

THE LOUVRE

KEY PAINTERS OF THE 20TH CENTURY

ARTIST	DATES	NATIONALITY	FAMOUS WORK	
Wassily Kandinsky	1866–1944	Russian	*Shrill-Peaceful Pink*	
Henri Matisse	1869–1954	French	*La danse*	
Pablo Picasso	1881–1973	Spanish	*Les demoiselles d'Avignon*	
Marc Chagall	1887–1985	Russian	*I and the Village*	
Salvador Dali	1904–1989	Spanish	*Premonition of a Civil War*	
Francis Bacon	1909–1992	English	*The Screaming Pope*	
Jackson Pollock	1912–1956	American	*Lavender Mist*	
Andy Warhol	1928–1987	American	*Marilyn*	 SALVADOR DALI

KEY PHOTOGRAPHERS OF THE 20TH CENTURY

	ARTIST	DATES	NATIONALITY	FORM
	Man Ray	1870–1976	American	Experimental
	Edward Weston	1886–1958	American	Still-life
	Ansel Adams	1902–1984	American	Landscape
	Walker Evans	1903–1975	American	Documentary
	Bill Brandt	1904–1983	English	Documentary
	Henri Cartier-Bresson	1908–	French	Photojournalism
	Robert Capa	1913–1954	Hungarian	Photojournalism
ANSEL ADAMS	Richard Avedon	1923–	American	Portraiture

KEY SCULPTORS OF THE 20TH CENTURY

ARTIST	DATES	NATIONALITY	FAMOUS WORK	
Constantin Brancusi	1876–1957	Romanian	*Torso of a Young Man*	
Jacob Epstein	1880–1959	American	*Ecce Homo*	
Hans Jean Arp	1887–1966	French	*Eggboard*	
Henry Moore	1898–1986	English	*Mother and Child*	
Alberto Giacometti	1901–1966	Italian	*Suspended Square*	
Barbara Hepworth	1903–1975	English	*Figure of a Woman*	
Anthony Caro	1924–	English	*Verduggio Sound*	
Eduardo Paolozzi	1924–	Scottish	*Medea*	
Jean Tinguely	1925–	Swiss	*Homage to New York*	
Andy Goldsworthy	1956–	English	*Ice Sculptures*	HENRY MOORE'S MOTHER AND CHILD

Theater, Film, and TV

The ancient Greeks are credited with inventing theater. In the last hundred years, technology has transformed stage drama into films, a massive industry based on moving pictures. It has also found ways to beam pictures into people's homes, in the form of television.

TECHNICOLOR CAMERA

WORLD TV VIEWING	
COUNTRY	HOURS PER WEEK
US	49.35
Italy	28.93
Hong Kong	28.70
Colombia	23.80
UK	23.80
Australia	21.98
Chile	17.50
China	10.59
Malaysia	10.50
World Average	19.67

FIRST COUNTRIES TO HAVE TELEVISION	
COUNTRY	YEAR
UK	1936
US	1939
USSR	1939
France	1948
Brazil	1950
Cuba	1950
Mexico	1950
Argentina	1951
Denmark	1951
Netherlands	1951

SHAKESPEARE FACTS

• William Shakespeare (1564 –1616), the English dramatist, is the most influential writer to have lived.

• He wrote 36 plays, 154 sonnets, and 2 narrative poems.

• His First Folio was published in 1623.

MOST OSCARS® WON	
NAME OF FILM	AWARDS
Ben Hur (1959)	11
West Side Story (1961)	10
Gigi (1958)	9
The Last Emperor (1987)	9
Gone With the Wind (1939)	8
Gandhi (1982)	8
From Here to Eternity (1953)	8
On the Waterfront (1954)	8
Cabaret (1972)	8
Amadeus (1984)	8

OSCAR®

KEY FILM DIRECTORS

NAME	DATE	NATIONALITY	KEY FILM
Fritz Lang	1890–1976	German	M (1930)
Jean Renoir	1894–1979	French	La règle du jeu (1939)
John Ford	1895–1973	American	Stagecoach (1939)
Sergei Eisenstein	1898–1948	Russian	Battleship Potemkin (1925)
Alfred Hitchcock	1899–1980	British	Psycho (1960)
Ingmar Bergman	1918–	Swedish	The Seventh Seal (1957)
Federico Fellini	1920–1993	Italian	La dolce vita (1959)
Satyajit Ray	1921–92	Indian	Pather Panchali (1955)
Stanley Kubrick	1928–	American	A Clockwork Orange (1971)
Francis Coppola	1939–	American	Apocalypse, Now! (1979)

DIRECTOR'S CHAIR

TOP US FILMS FROM EACH DECADE*

FILM	YEAR	APPROX. RENTAL
Jurassic Park	1993	$208,000,000
ET, the Extra-Terrestrial	1983	$228,200,000
Star Wars	1977	$193,800,000
The Sound of Music	1965	$80,000,000
The Ten Commandments	1956	n/a
Bambi	1942	n/a
Gone With the Wind	1939	$79,400,000

* Highest-grossing video rentals

ORIENTAL THEATER

• Japanese *kabuki* evolved in the late 17th century. It combines stylized acting with singing, dancing, and elaborate costumes and makeup.

• Indian *kathakali* trains its actors in the art of facial expression. This conveys all aspects of the story being told.

• Indonesian shadow theater uses puppets, a narrator, and music to tell traditional folk tales.

JAVANESE SHADOW PUPPET

KEY 20TH-CENTURY PLAYWRIGHTS

NAME	DATE	NATIONALITY	PLAY
George Bernard Shaw	1856–1950	Irish	Pygmalion
Eugene O'Neill	1888–1953	American	Strange Interlude
Bertolt Brecht	1898–1956	German	Threepenny Opera
Samuel Beckett	1906–89	Irish	Waiting for Godot
Tennessee Williams	1911–83	American	The Glass Menagerie
Arthur Miller	1915–	American	Death of a Salesman
John Osborne	1929–1994	British	Look Back in Anger
Harold Pinter	1930–	British	The Caretaker

Music and dance

Both forms of expression have their origins in ancient religious ritual. In some parts of the world, people still dance themselves into trances to communicate with spirits; elsewhere, musical concerts and dance performances of many different kinds continue to keep audiences spellbound.

FAMOUS BALLETS

TITLE	CHOREOGRAPHER	FIRST DANCED
Les sylphides	Filippo Taglionii (1777–1871), Italian	1832
Nutcracker	Lev Ivanov (1834–1901), Russian	1892
Swan Lake	Lev Ivanov and Marius Petipa (1818–1910), French	1895
Manon	Kenneth MacMillan(1929–1993), British	1974

WORLD DANCE STYLES

EUROPE
Many traditional European folk dances have their roots in religious ritual.

NATIVE AMERICAN
Dancing takes place at special ceremonies to win the goodwill of gods and ancestor spirits.

EAST ASIA
Dance is central to the main theatrical dramas. Japanese gagaku is one of the oldest traditional court dances.

SOUTHEAST ASIA
Highly trained artists perform slow, classical dances with complex hand movements.

AFRICA
Dance reflects the tribal roots of Sun and Moon worship, as well as hunt and fertility dances.

INDIA
Dancing re-enacts the ancient religious epics of gods and men.

INDIAN DANCER

KEY DANCE STYLES

BALLET
Ballet uses formalized dancing, choreographed to music, to tell a story. Its main styles are modern, romantic, and classical.

TAP
Tap dance is characterized by tapping the heel and toe of the shoe on the floor to create rhythms.

CALYPSO
Caribbean carnivals were the birthplaces of calypso. This street dance is usually accompanied by steel-band percussion.

WALTZ
At first labeled immoral, the waltz changed dancing with its fast, turning movements and the close embrace of the dancers.

FLAMENCO
Derived from the old gypsy dances of southern Spain, flamenco is spontaneous and emotive.

KEY CLASSICAL COMPOSERS

NAME	NATIONALITY/ DATES	FAMOUS WORKS
Antonio Vivaldi	Italian, 1678–1741	*The Four Seasons*
Johann Sebastian Bach	German, 1685–1750	*Brandenburg Concertos, St. Matthew Passion*
George Frederic Handel	German, 1685–1759	*The Messiah, Music for the Royal Fireworks*
Wolfgang Amadeus Mozart	Austrian, 1756–1791	*Piano Concerto in C major, Mass in C minor*
Ludwig van Beethoven	German, 1770–1827	*Symphonies No. 3, No. 5, and No. 9*
Franz Schubert	Austrian, 1797–1828	*Die Winterreise, Symphony No. 8 "Unfinished"*
Hector Berlioz	French, 1803–1869	*Symphonie fantastique, The Trojans*
Richard Wagner	German, 1813–1883	*The Flying Dutchman, The Ride of the Valkyries*
Peter Ilyich Tchaikovsky	Russian, 1840–1893	*Swan Lake, The Sleeping Beauty, The Nutcracker*
Claude Debussy	French, 1862–1918	*L'Après-midi d'un faune, La mer, Images*
Arnold Schoenberg	Austrian, 1874–1951	*Transfigured Night, A Survivor from Warsaw*

KEY MUSICAL STYLES

FOLK MUSIC
This broad term applies to traditional, community-based music. Each society has its own form.

BLUES
Basically simple, hugely influential, melancholic songs created by poor black minorities.

JAZZ
Born in the US in the early 1900s, when musicians began to improvise around popular music themes.

POP
A 1950s term meaning any song or piece of music with mass appeal, usually with a danceable beat.

REGGAE
Beat music with a distinctive rhythm that originated in the West Indies in the early 1960s.

ROCK
A combination of various forms of black popular music with a heavy beat pioneered in the US and UK.

COUNTRY
The "white man's blues," country music now also embraces urban themes and styles.

TECHNO
Based around a rapid 4/4 beat and electronic sounds, this style first became popular in the 1980s.

KEY OPERAS

TITLE	COMPOSER	FIRST PERFORMED
The Marriage of Figaro	Wolfgang Amadeus Mozart (1756–1791), Austrian	1786, Vienna, Austria
The Barber of Seville	Gioacchino Rossini (1792–1868), Italian	1816, Rome, Italy
The Ring of the Nibelung	Richard Wagner (1813–1883), German	1876, Bayreuth, Germany
La Bohème	Giacomo Puccini (1858–1924), Italian	1896, Turin, Italy

OPERA SINGER

RAT
1996

OX
1997

TIGER
1998

RABBIT
1999

DRAGON
2000

SNAKE
2001

HORSE
2002

GOAT
2003

MONKEY
2004

COCKEREL
2005

DOG
2006

PIG
2007

CALENDARS

THE PASSAGE OF TIME, beginning with the cycle of seasons, was civilization's first obsession. The ancient Maya devoted themselves to the "long count," using complex mathematics and astronomy. With these methods, other societies have calculated their own calendars.

THE SEASONS		
NORTHERN HEMISPHERE	SOUTHERN HEMISPHERE	DURATION
Spring	Autumn	From vernal/ autumnal equinox (c. Mar. 21) to summer/ winter solstice (c. Jun. 21)
Summer	Winter	From summer/ winter solstice (c. Jun. 21) to autumnal/ spring equinox (c. Sept. 23)
Autumn	Spring	From autumnal/ spring equinox (c. Sept. 23) to winter/ summer solstice (c. Dec. 21)
Winter	Summer	From winter/ summer solstice (c. Dec. 21) to vernal/ autumnal equinox (c. Mar. 21)

NAMES OF THE DAYS		
DAY	NAME ORIGIN	SATURN
Sunday	Sun day	
Monday	Moon day	
Tuesday	Tiw's day (God of battle)	
Wednesday	Woden's or Odin's day (God of poetry and the dead)	
Thursday	Thor's day (God of thunder)	
Friday	Frigg's day (Goddess of married love)	
Saturday	Saturn's day (God of time)	

EXPLANATION OF CALENDARS

JULIAN/ GREGORIAN
The Julian calendar calculated the solar year at 365 days, divided into 12 months. In 1582, Pope Gregory XII adjusted a 10-day gap that had gathered between this calendar and the astronomical year.

CHINESE
The ancient Chinese calendar is based on the lunar year and has 12 months of alternatively 29 and 30 days. Each year is signified by an animal. A cycle passes through each one of the signs before returning to the start.

ISLAMIC
The Islamic calendar is based on the lunar year and runs in cycles of 30 years. It begins with the year of Hijrah (AD 622), the flight of Muhammad to Medina.

JEWISH
The Jewish calendar is based on the lunar year and consists of 12 months of 29 or 30 days. An extra month is added to 7 years of every 19-year cycle to bring the calendar back in time with the solar year.

JEWISH CANDLE HOLDER

MONTH OF THE YEAR

GREGORIAN	JEWISH	ISLAMIC	ZODIAC
(Basis : Sun)	(Basis: Moon)	(Basis: Moon)*	(Basis: Sun)
January	Shevat (Jan–Feb)	Jumada I	Capricorn (Dec. 22–Jan. 20)
February	Adar (Feb–Mar)	Jumada II	Aquarius (Jan. 21–Feb. 18)
March	Adar Sheni –leap years only	Rajab	Pisces (Feb. 19–Mar. 20)
April	Nisan (Mar–Apr)	Shaban	Aries (Mar. 21–Apr. 20)
May	Iyar (Apr–May)	Ramadan	Taurus (Apr. 21–May 21)
June	Sivan (May–Jun)	Shawwal	Gemini (May 22–Jun. 21)
July	Tammuz (Jun–Jul)	Dhu al-Qadah	Cancer (Jun. 22–July 22)
August	Av (Jul–Aug)	Dhu al Hijja	Leo (July 23–Aug. 23)
September	Elul (Aug–Sep)	Muharram	Virgo (Aug. 24–Sep. 22)
October	Tishri (Sep–Oct)	Safar	Libra (Sep. 23–Oct. 23)
November	Heshvan (Oct–Nov)	Rabi 1	Scorpio (Oct. 24–Nov. 22)
December	Kislev (Nov–Dec)	Rabi II	Sagittarius (Nov. 23–Dec.21)
	Tevet (Dec–Jan)	* No leap years– months change date each year.	

Index

Acknowledgements

Dorling Kindersley would like to thank:
Hilary Bird for the index; Louise Cox for
design assistance; the Science Museum;
Caroline Potts for picture library services;
Chris Jackson and Dave Roberts for
cartographic assistance.

Illustrations by:
Russell Barnett, Richard Blakely, Richard
Bonson, Peter Bull, Kuo Kang Chen,
Luciano Corbella, Brian Delf, William
Donohue, Eugene Fluery, Roy Flookes,
Bob Garwood, Will Giles, Mike Grey, Nick
Hall, Nick Heweston, Colette Ho, Bruce
Hogarth, John Hutchinson, Richard Lewis,
Mick Loates/Linden Artists, Judith
Maguire, Janos Marfy, Kate Miller, Richard
Platt, Sandra Pond, Sabastian Quigley,
J. Robins, Colin Rose, Colin Salmon,
Rodney Shackell, Roger Stewart, John
Temperton, Richard Ward,
John Woodcock.

Photographs by:
Peter Chadwick, Geoff Dann, Philip
Dowell, Mike Dunning, Peter Hayman,
Chas Howson, Gary Kevin, Dave King,
Neil Lukas, Eric Meacher, Ray Moller,
Steve Oliver, Dave Rudkin, Kim Sayer,
Clive Steeter, Jane Stockman.

Picture credits:
The publisher would like to thank the
following for their kind permission to
reproduce their photographs:

t=top b=bottom c=centre l=left r=righ
© Acadamy of Motion Picture Arts and
Sciences ®: 116 br; British Museum: 56
Bureau Internationale des Poids et
Mesures, Sèvres: 96 cl; Corbis/ Bettman/
UPI: 115 cl; Eurostar/ European Passenge
Services/ de Souza: 65 tl; Mary Evans
Picture Library: 120 br; Glasgow Museum
The Burrell Collection: 121 t ; The Rona
Grant Archive: 73 tl; Robert Harding
Picture Library: 49 tl, Nigel Francis 38 tl
60–61, Adam Woolfit 102–103; IBM:
72 bl; The Image Bank: George Obremsk
52 tl, Harald Sund 53 br, Terry Williams
cl, Imperial War Museum: 59 tr; © The
Henry Moore Foundation: Michael Mull
115 br; Museum of Artillery: 58 tl; NAS
13 tr,14 l, 15 tl, 18 bl, 18 cl, 77 br; Rex
Features Ltd: Patrick Frilet 51 br; Tony
Stone Images: 100 tl; United Nations:
32–33; Wallace Collection: 58 r

Every effort has been made to trace the
copyright holders and we apologize in
advance for any unintentional omissions
We would be pleased to insert the
appropriate acknowledgement in any
subsequent edition of this publication.